Elfie Wilkins-Nacht

The Hawai'ian Paintings

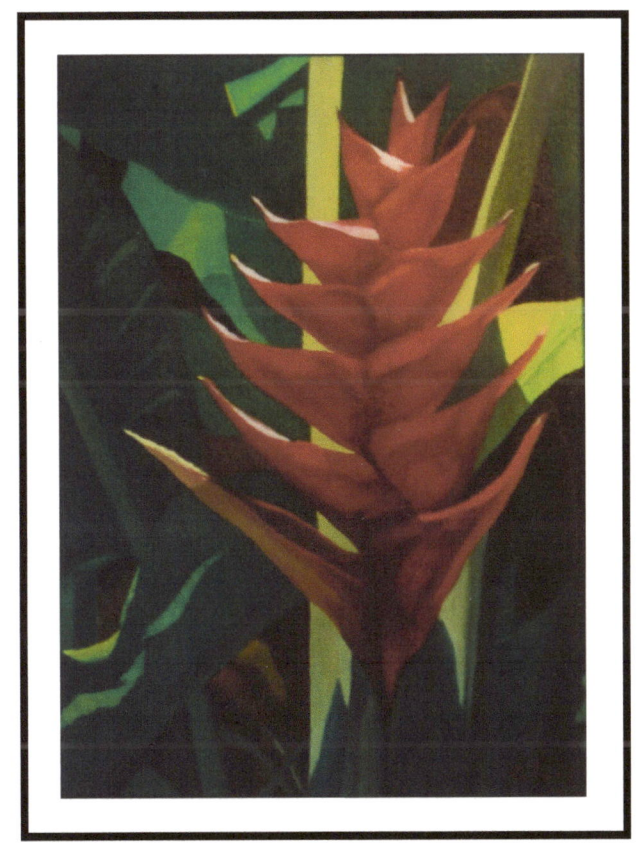

IMAGE ON COVER

"SEALING WAX PALM"
Oil painting 30 x 42 inches.   2004
Private collection

TITLE PAGE IMAGE

"HELICONIA"
Oil painting 16 x 20 inches.   2005
Collection of Lena Higa

From the Director's Desk

      Elfie Wilkins-Nacht is well known in Hawai`i for her luxurious floral paintings. What one is struck by when first viewing these works is the confident eye of the painter whose background as a photographer has lent itself masterfully to these compositions. Her unerring eye brings the viewer intimately into a relationship with the subject of her paintings inspiring awe at Nature's marvelous ability to bring into being the diverse, sometimes exotic, wonders of the natural world. Elfie Wilkins-Nacht takes what surrounds us every day and makes us realize how beautiful and extraordinary our world is. Whether it is a branch of Ginkgo or the entire Hawaiian landscape her ability to embrace and enhance her view of the world imbues these paintings with rich color, perfectly executed forms and like a poet working with words Elfie Wilkins-Nacht takes her painterly elements creating a sonnet to the world of flowers and Nature that she loves and wishes to share with others.

      Elfie who was born in Italy grew up in a world where the influence of classical painting was evident everywhere. One only had to look in churches or other public buildings where Italian art was present creating a lasting impression on the viewer. Milano a city where almost every master painter in Western Art is represented was Elfie's playground. As a child she was well aware of the colors and forms, the subject matter of the frescoes in the churches when her family attended mass every Sunday.

      As an adult Elfie moved to the United States and to California in particular where she continued painting for her pleasure. It was her husband, Robert who encouraged her to take extended education classes in Santa Monica where they lived. It was here that Elfie got her first formal training in painting. After applying to UCLA as an undergraduate student Elfie studied painting and other art disciplines. Even though she was a UCLA graduate student in Photography she continued to paint using her photography for the basis of her paintings.

      It wasn't until she came to Hawai`i that Elfie really embraced oil painting with a fervor that demanded all of her attention. Struck by the beauty all around her she felt challenged by the forms and colors inspiring her to create this wonderful body of work.

Lourdan Kimbrell, President/Director
Hawaii Museum of Contemporary Art

Elfie Wilkins-Nacht

I was born into a very creative Swiss family. My aunt, Frida, a piano player, made a living by playing for guests at hotels, another aunt played well enough to perform in a church while in Milano, my mother played the piano at the cinema for silent movies. Among my cousins there were singers, a violinist, and a visual artist, Leni, who painted by commission and made a living in Zurich decorating window displays. Once I reached adulthood, my mother more than once told me that the reason why I excel in the art was because I was in her belly when she, in Milano, was painting faces on small statuettes that my father and his partner cast in plaster and alabaster. They had a shop but slowly during World War II the business collapsed. When when my father died the shop was closed down.

Milano, the most industrial city in Italy was the target of the British Air Force and toward the end of the war the planes would come nightly to drop bombs all around us. People at that time had difficulty finding food. They were in a survival mode. Grownups would complain that the milk was watered down and that they found rat's tails in the salami. I even heard that the bread had marble powder in it to make it weigh more. Growing up I was left often alone since both parents were out working. I had plenty of time playing with dolls and making up plots with my imaginary sisters. I had seven of them and each one had a specific trait. I would talk to my "Sisters" scolding if necessary and so on. What I was doing is now called "creative play." After my father died my mother, now a widow, had no job; only my brother, who was 20 at the time, had one. I was a child of seven we were poor but strangely enough I was not aware of our situation. While my mother was looking for a job she was able to rent out one of our master bedrooms. That helped for awhile but not enough because she took one of her sisters advice and we returned to Switzerland where my mother spent her childhood and youth.

It was in Switzerland that our family life became more settled. After junior high I began to work helping out with the family finances. I also began to have some spending money. I enjoyed the art classes that we had in school and the teachers gave me good grades. I don't remember how I learned to mix oil paints or what kind of medium I used to mix them. In any case I taught myself how to paint in oils. I just know how much satisfaction that act of painting gave me, thus every free weekend I would do so. I painted flowers, still life, and a large sailing ship. That to me, in retrospect announced my long voyage to the United States.

In 1963 I joined my husband, Robert, in California and was busy taking ESL classes 36 hours a week at USC.. I enjoyed that tremendously because learning for me, is my goal in life. I began to paint again when I became pregnant with my daughter, Jessica. Without formal lessons I painted "Girl in the Field", which was quite large. When my husband noticed that I was skillful at painting he suggested that I take evening art classes in Santa Monica. He also insisted that I take them for a grade. I laughed at him. " There is no way I can enter college at my age, I told him" However, I did take the classes and for a grade. I became very grateful that I followed his advice once I finished my education with a MFA in photography at UCLA.

Elfie

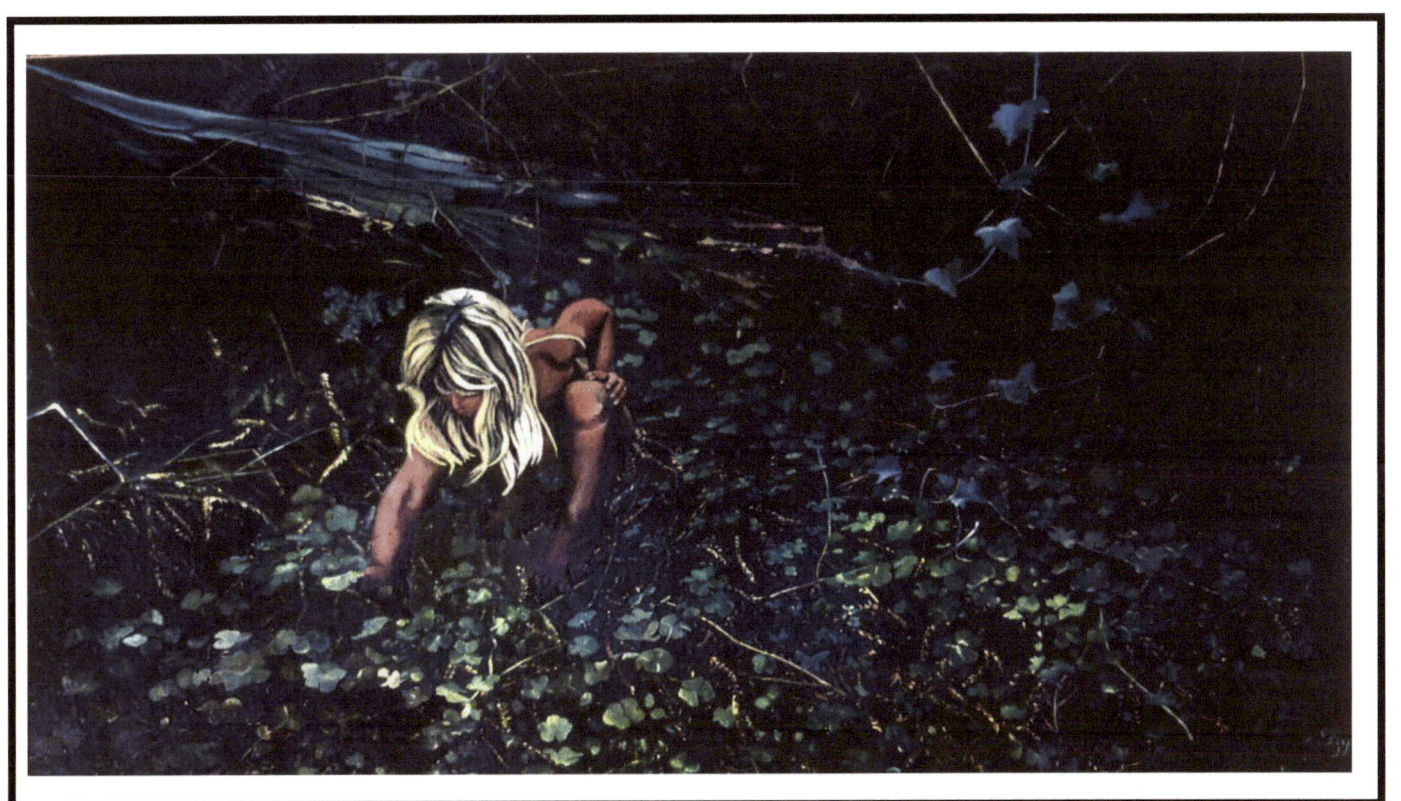

"GIRL IN THE FIELD"
Oil painting, 68 x 48 inches.   1963

We Move to Hawai`i

When my husband, Robert, decided to retire he wanted to find a less hectic lifestyle, less traffic and pollution. He remembered how much fun our family had while visiting Hawai`i in 1976 when we came to swim the 2 1/4 mile Waikiki Ocean Swim. Years later, my husband decided to return and check out the other islands. When he returned from his trip he informed me that he was negotiating on a very nice ocean-front property on Molokai. I was speechless. I told him that there wasn't a hospital, university or library on Molokai so how was I going to get a teaching job? Fate intervened. The seller wouldn't come down on the price and another interested buyer paid the full price for the property. My husband then traveled to Hawai`i staying in a van, circling the island until he discovered Keaukaha where he found a property near Richardson Beach Park that he liked and purchased it. He moved ahead of me in order to begin building our house and I arrived in 1993 finding that I liked the location very much. I had never been to the island of Hawai`i or to Hilo until I joined my husband, Robert there in 1993. We traveled around the island to familiarize ourselves with the area and to visit the historic places.

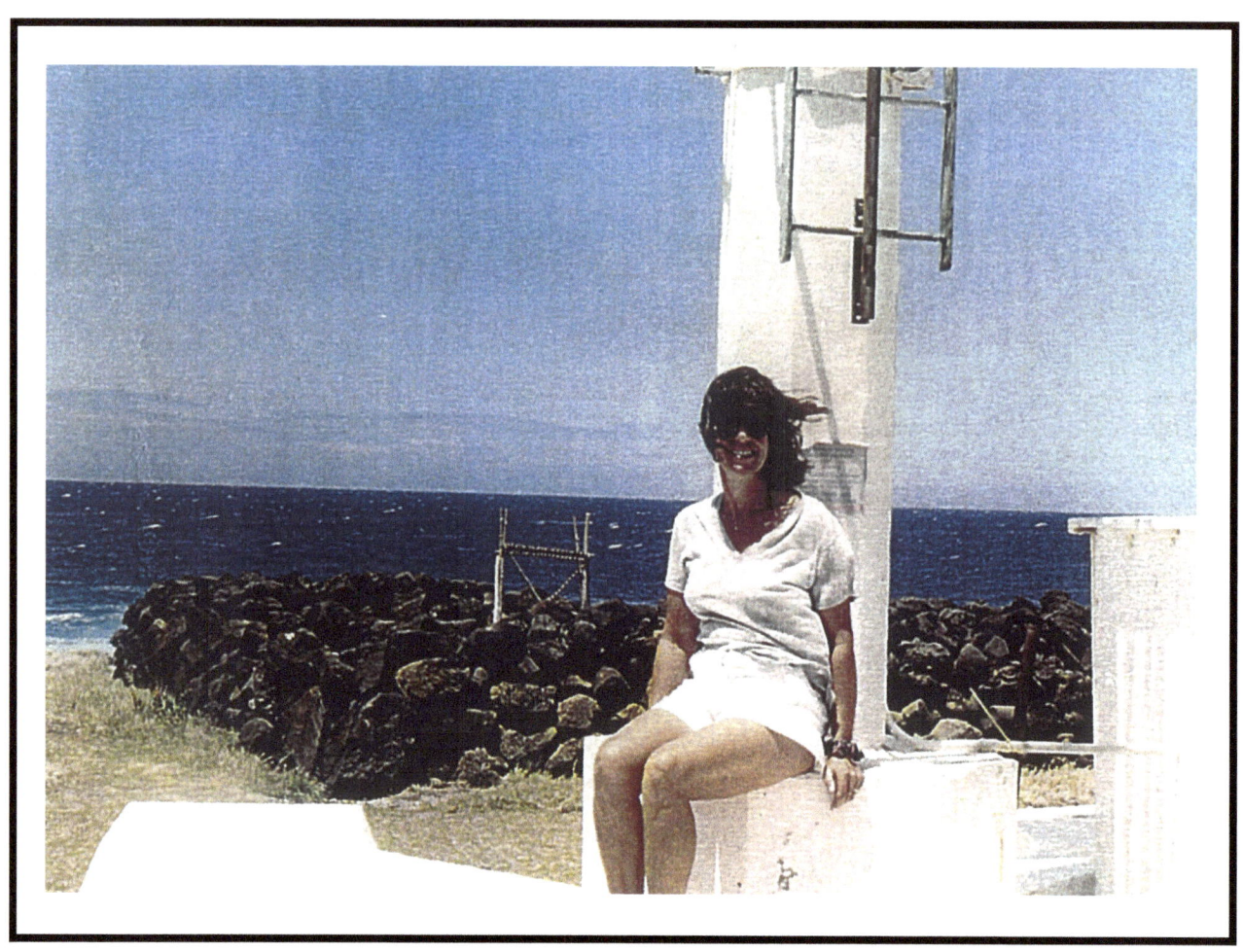

Here I am at South Point, 1993. The photo was taken by my husband Robert.

When we reached South Point there was a strong wind blowing that according to the people who lived there was not unusual. A crooked, battered tree there caught my attention as it had the appearance of a giant Bonsai tree shaped by Nature. A week or so later when I had the photo of the tree in my hand I decided to do a painting of the tree in oils. To me the tree symbolized the rough beauty of South Point. The painting was in a juried show at the Hawaii Museum of Contemporary Art in 1996. When Barbara Williams saw it she bought it because it reminded her of the trees she had seen in Africa.

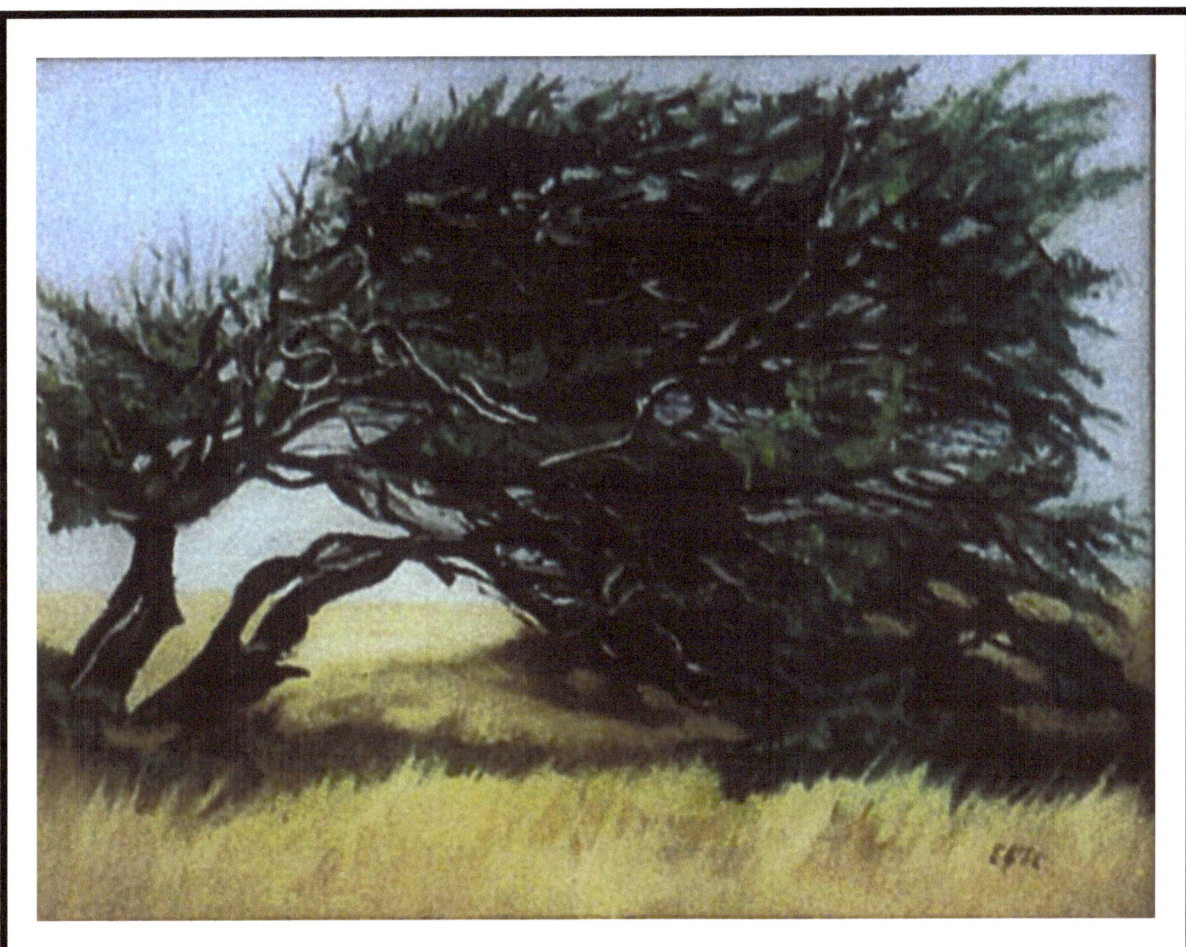

"SOUTH POINT"
Oil painting on canvas, 11 x 14 inches.   2007
Collection of Barbara Williams

Every plant and flower on this island is spectacular. I always was attracted to flowers, plants and Nature in general. I like to paint in a naturalistic way by looking for the lights and darks. Johannes Vermeer, the Dutch painter who specialized in domestic interior scenes of Dutch life is one of my favorite artists because he remained truthful to what he saw in front of him. He did not need to add pretty colors to his work for the sake of prettiness. His paintings of interiors reflect the natural beauty of light falling on his subjects. I have painted gardenias with subtle tonal gradations, Heliconia, African Tulip flowers with striking shapes and vivid colors. Fan palms are one of my favorite subjects. I paint them in a semi-abstract manner so I can emphasize Nature's perfect patterns and shapes. Cane grass with the long blades and the intense green color has also become one of my favorite plants to paint. I dislike painting a subject that I have already painted as it would only be a mechanical exercise lacking the passion and excitement I experience by painting something new.

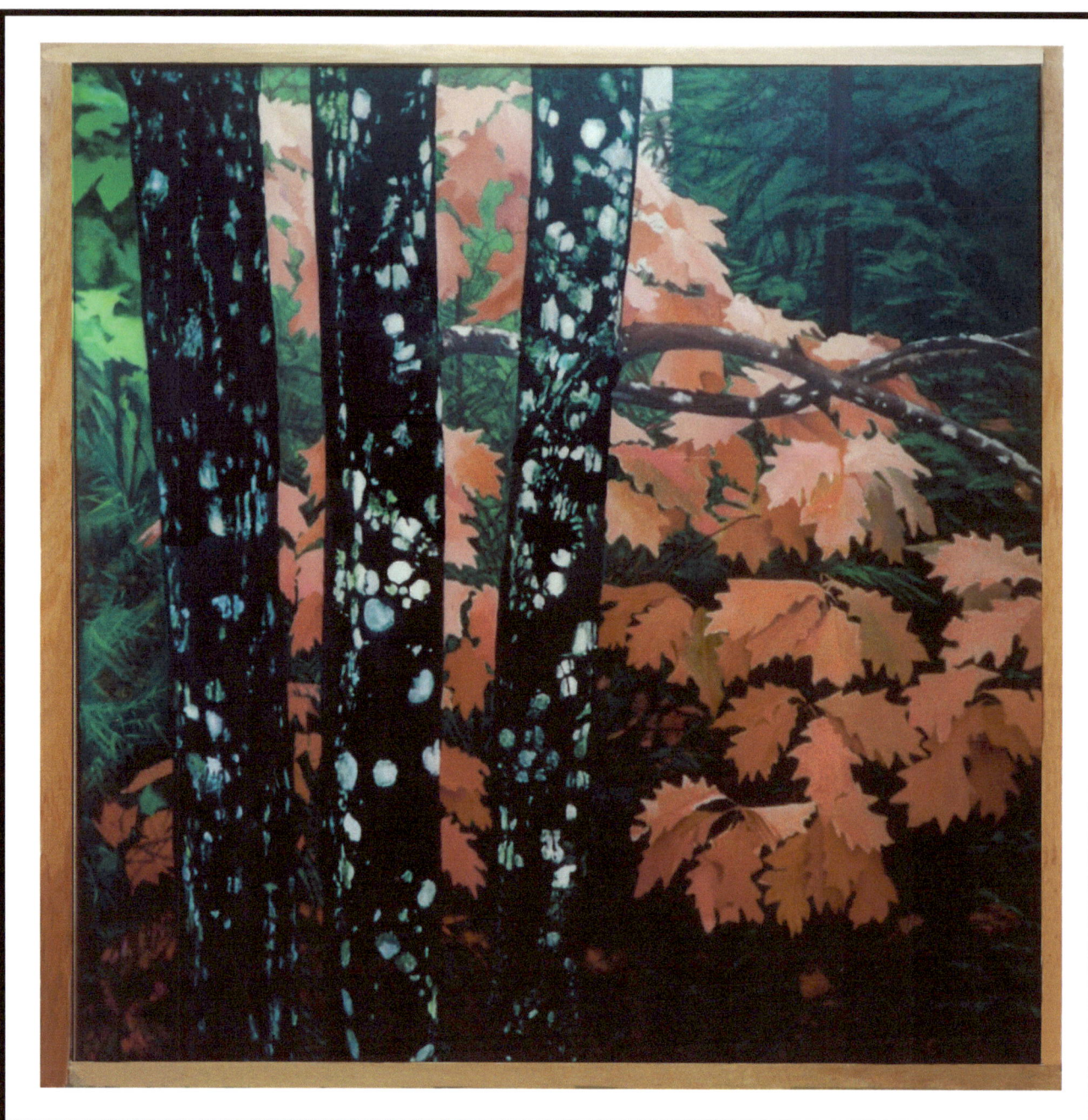

"PEEK-A-BOO"
Oil painting, 40 x40 inches.   1997
Collection of Ms. Claire Kaneshiro, Amman, Jordan

I could not resist painting the gorgeous foliage playing hide and seek behind the spotted tree bark. This is one of the first large paintings I did in Hilo, Hawai'i. I had difficulty with those light colored spots on the tree bark so that the perspective would look natural as they go around the tree trunk. I applied a mixture of paint and painting medium to most of the leaves. For this painting I constructed the frame with 1 x 2 inch wood and stained it a medium brown. The transparent stain allowed the pattern of the wood to show through. I was doubtful that anyone would buy it because it is not a Hawaiian subject but a scene from the mainland. When the painting hung outside the entrance of the gallery "Art at the Ironworks", for my upcoming exhibition ,a visitor from Amman, Jordan saw it and bought it.

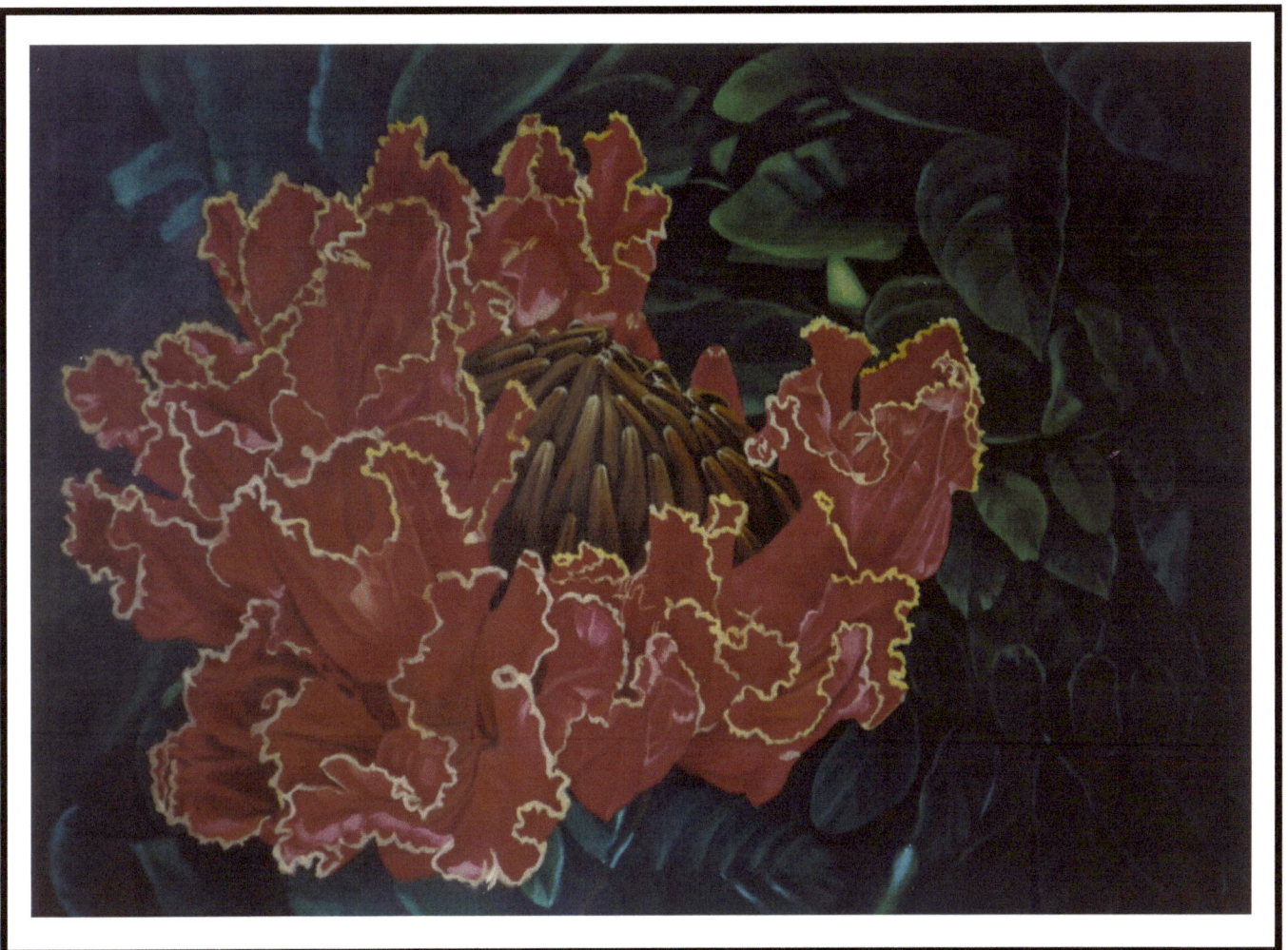

"AFRICAN TULIP"
Oil painting, 28 x 28 inches.   1997
Private Collection

I have always loved flowers. My Mother always had some fresh flowers around our home. When I came to Hawai'i I never expected that the flowers here could be so different from the ones I saw in Europe or the mainland. The peculiar shapes, the bright colors in some and the very delicate ones in others plus the most amazing sizes of some of them intrigued me. They were so unfamiliar to me that I wanted to own some of them so I began to plant flowers and plants searching at plant sales for ones that I didn't have then going to the library to learn where best to plant them and where they come from. When my African Tulip Tree began to bloom I noticed that the blossoms would open one-at-a-time, first on the outside then the inside circle. The flower was so spectacular in shape and color that I began to take photos of it. One day my neighbor came over I guess to see what I was doing and he said to me, "You should get rid of that trash tree." "They are just a nuisance." I had never heard that expression, "Trash Tree" before. "Trees are trees." I thought. So I decided to honor the African Tulip Tree by painting one of its blossoms very large. Of course I also wanted to see if I could capture those reddish orange tones and all of the details of the flowers and leaves.

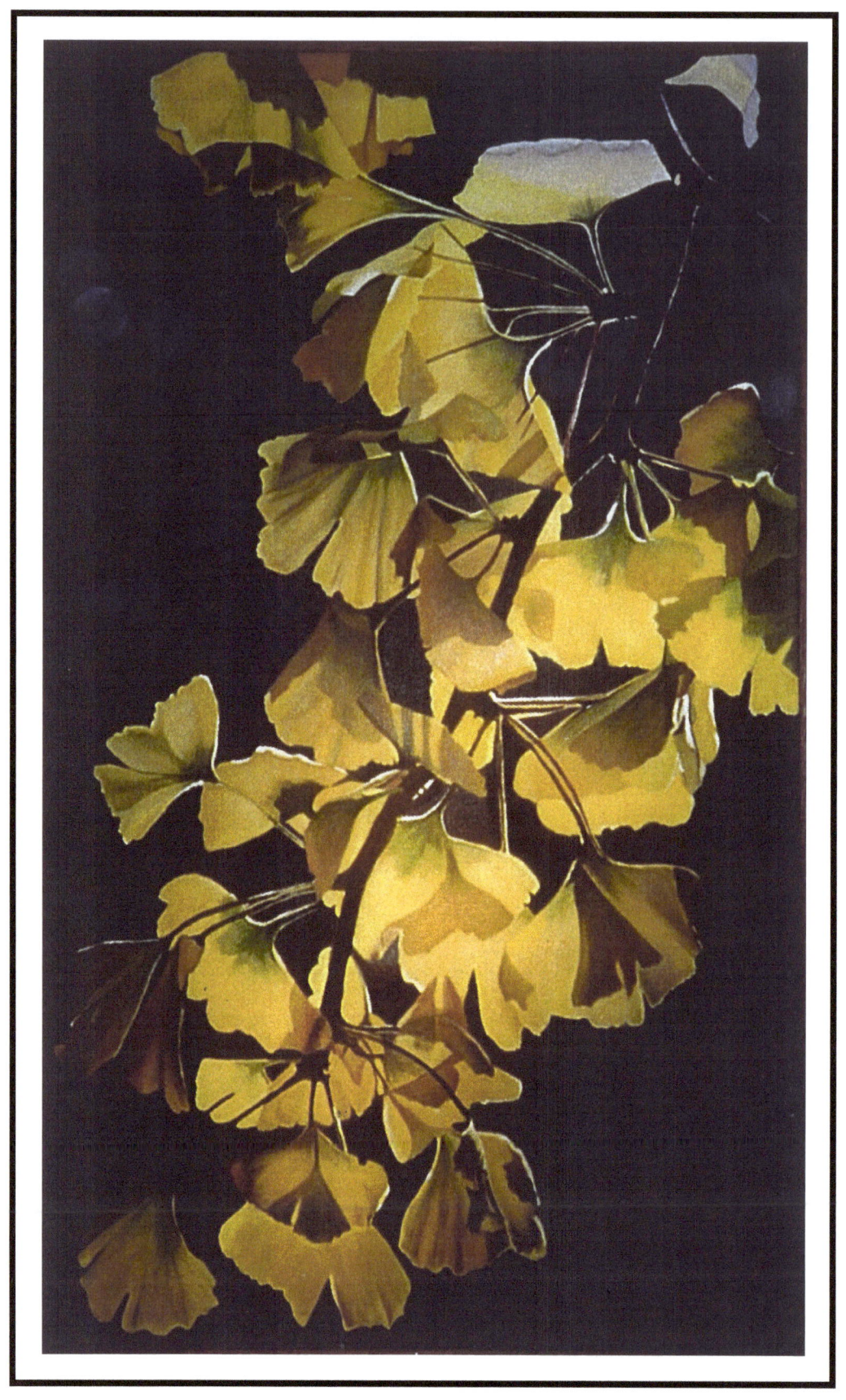

"GOLDEN GINKGO"
Oil on canvas, 40 X 24 Inches. 2000
Collection of Dr. Mary Graner

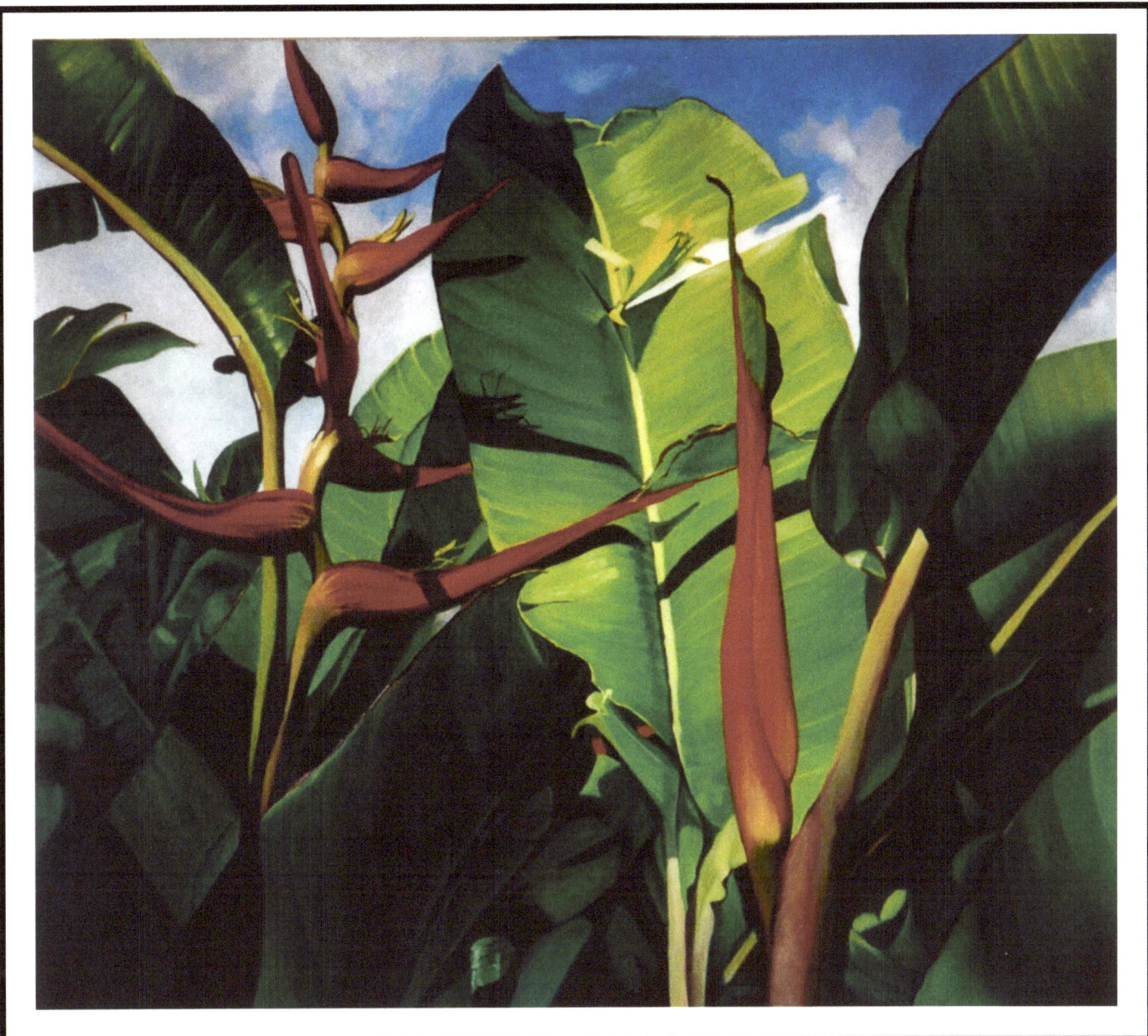

"SCARLET HELICONIA"
Oil on canvas, 42 x 48 inches.   1998
Private collection

I like the challenge of painting very large works. Doing so forces me to keep my enthusiasm for the subject from the beginning of the process until the end which isn't easy to sustain. There is a story behind this painting that is interesting now but wasn't when I was in the process of painting this picture. I was holding a two-inch wide stainless steel ruler and somehow let it slip out of my hand and it landed on the painting slashing the canvas. The painting was half-finished and I was so upset that I was ready to discard it. Later, I decided to try to repair it so I glued a piece of canvas onto the back where the slit was and it looked alright to me. A couple of days later my friend, Maryanka, came for a visit and saw the painting. I asked her to look closely at the work and see if she noticed anything strange about it. She could not. I offered to sell her the painting at a reduced price. She liked it so much she bought it.

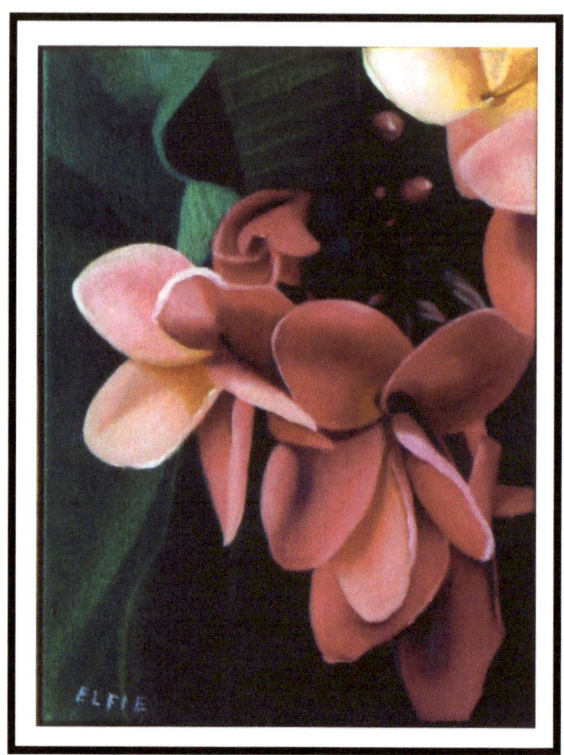

"PLUMERIA IV"
Oil painting, 12 x 9 inches.   2012
Private collection

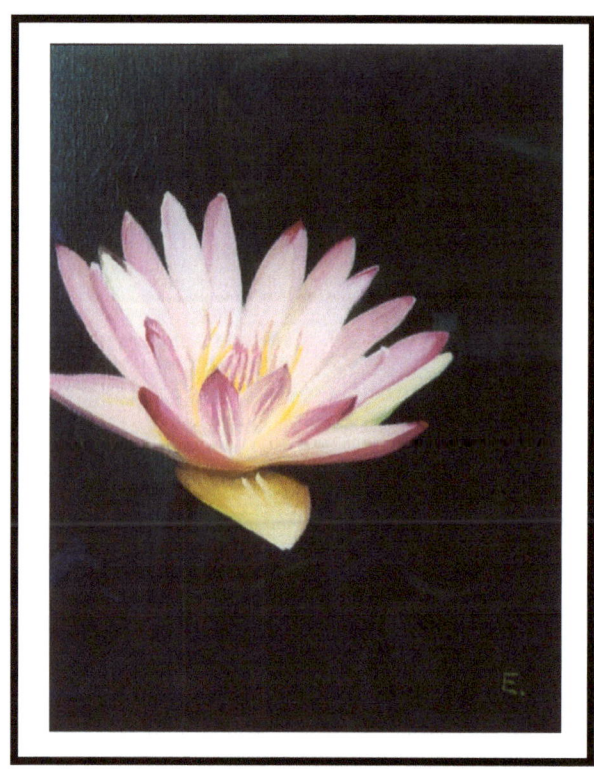

"LILY PADS"
Oil painting, 9 x 12 inches.   2005
Private collection

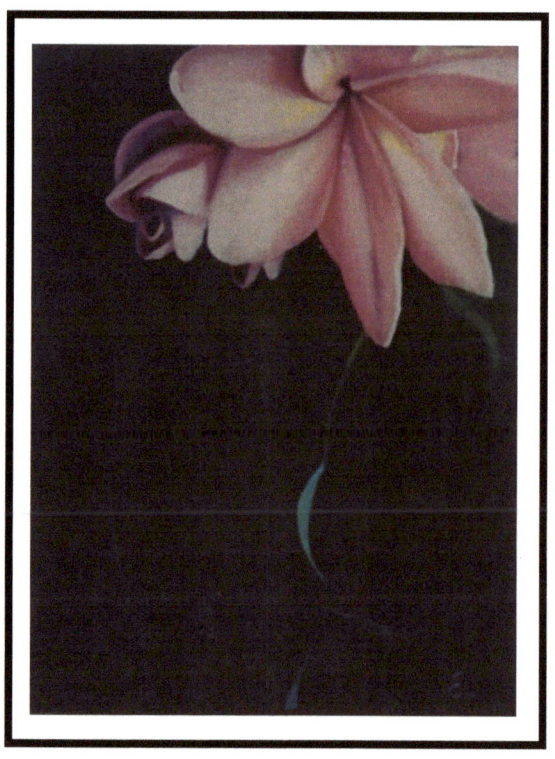

"PLUMERIA"
Oil painting,
Private collection

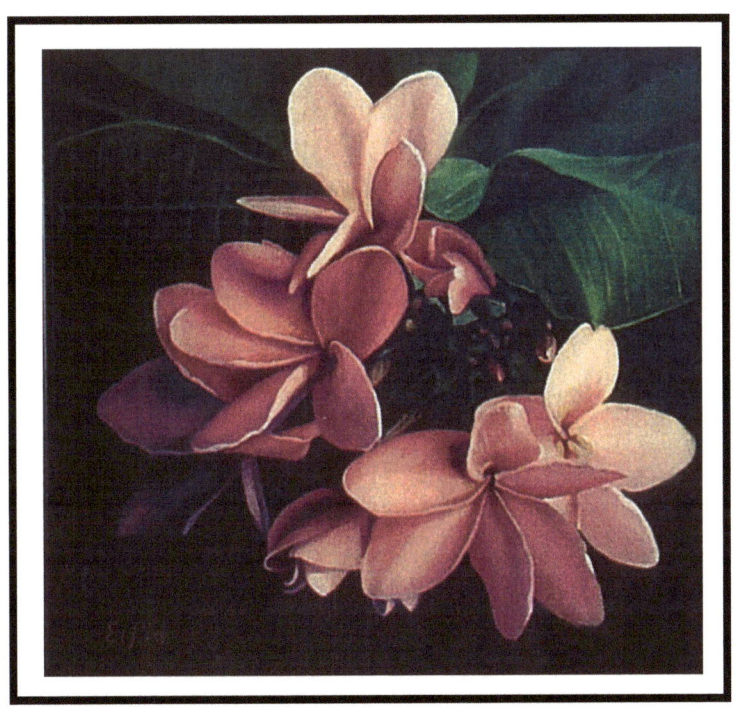

"PLUMERIA III"
Oil painting, 16 x 20 inches.   2006
Collection of L. McDonald & Hope N.

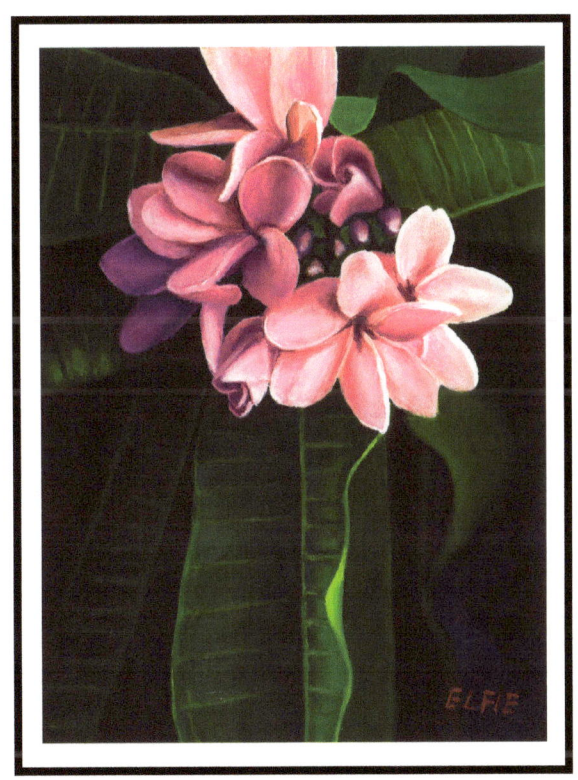

"PLUMERIA V"
Oil painting, 12 x 9 inches.   2013
Collection of Lourdan Kimbrell

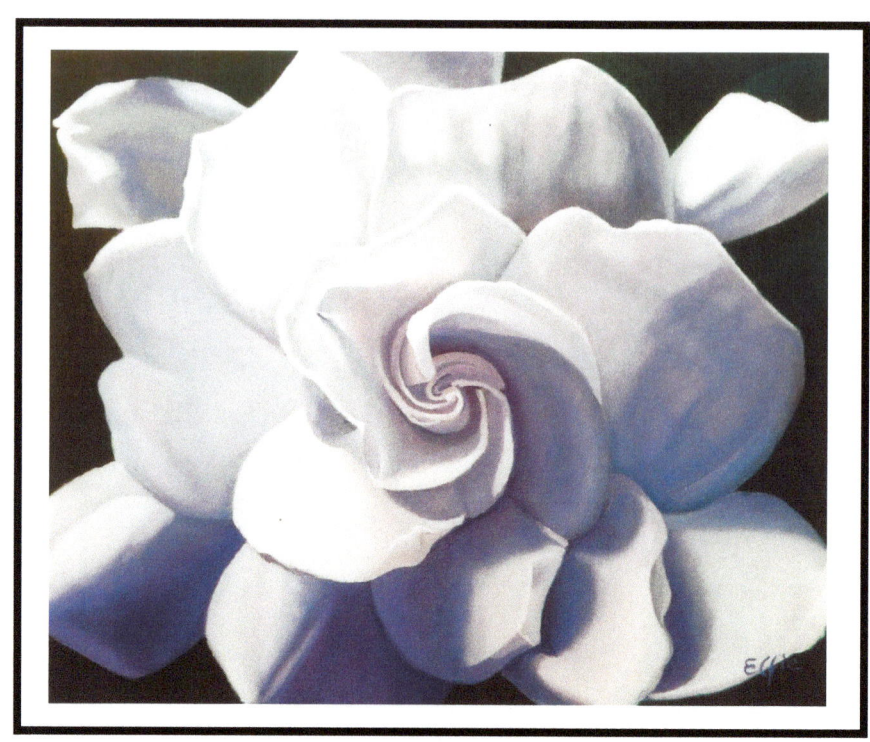

"GARDENIA II"
Oil painting, 20 X 24 inches.   2008
Collection of Mrs. Alyce Arata

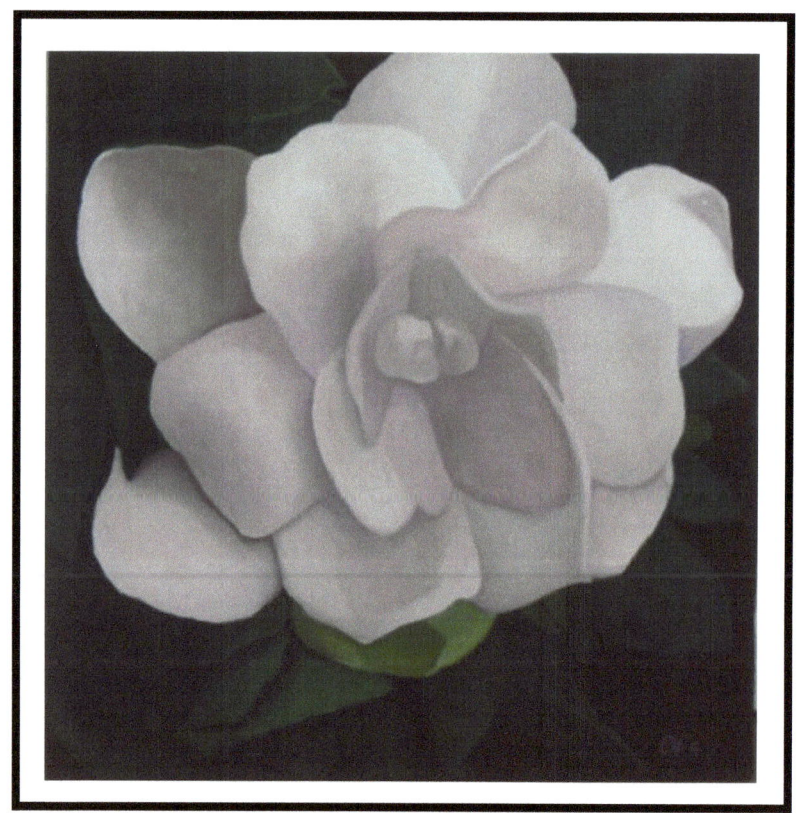

"GARDENIA I"
Oil painting, 20 x 20 inches   2008
Private collection

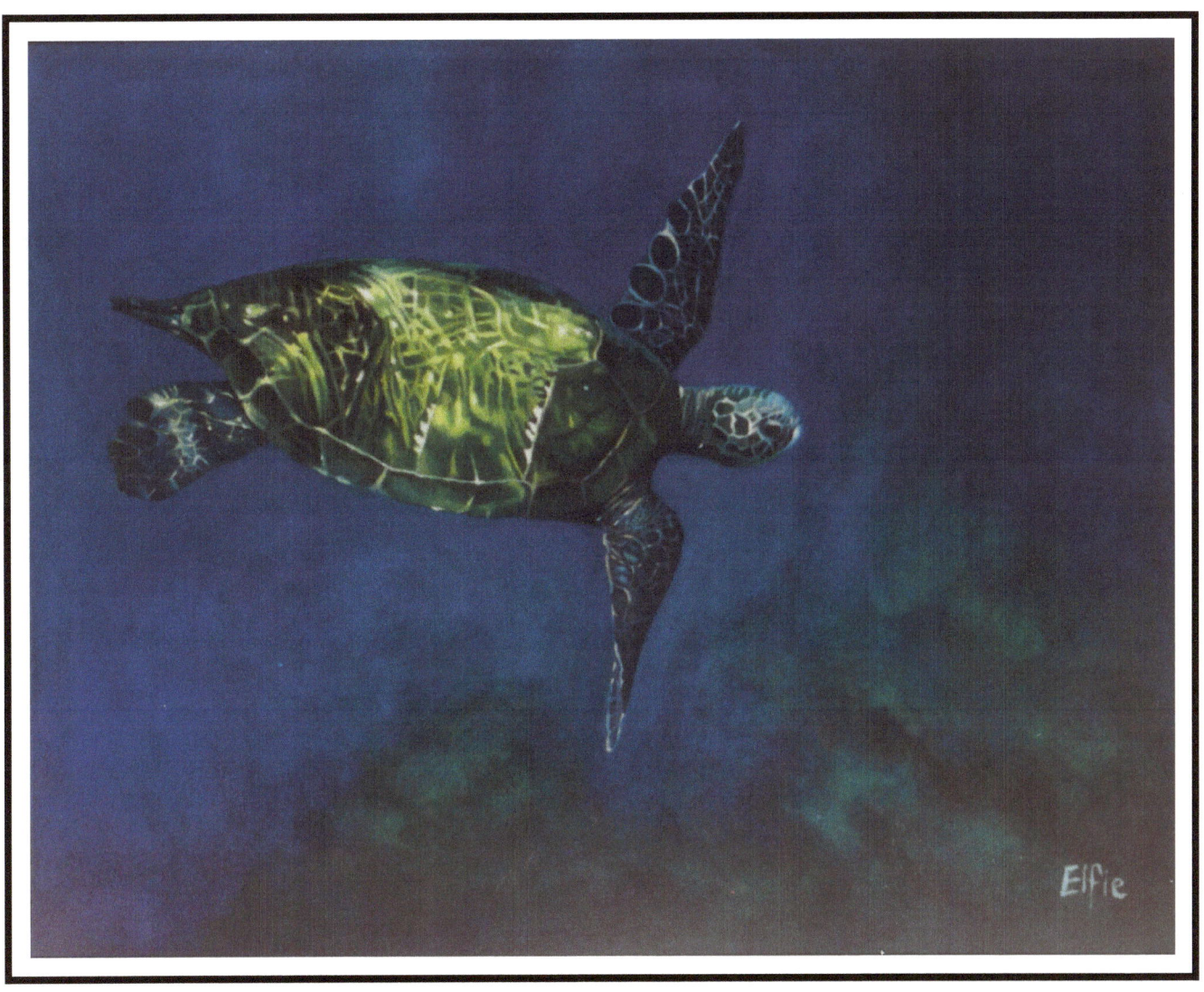

"HONU"
Oil painting, 34 x 45 inches,   2003
Collection of the artist

This is a large painting, 34 by 45 inches, that we still have hanging in our home. My husband, Robert took this photo of a Honu (turtle in Hawaiian) at Richardson Beach Park in Hilo outside of the breakwater where he has been swimming since we came to this island twenty-three years ago. This work was painted with many coats of glaze (a mixture of pigments and painting medium). I was curious about how many layers of medium would be needed to satisfy me. I counted twenty-seven coats of medium each with transparent color: Ultramarine, Prussian, Manganese Blue, Viridian and Alizarin Crimson added to it. Underneath the oil painting there are areas of "Under-painting White", a sort of textural paste specifically used with oil paint so that a painter can simulate textures of rocks, tree bark or other things. I am always attracted by the light in any particular subject for the way it creates tonal differentiations in the colors. That is also the reason I prefer to paint on large canvases as it is easier to blend tones to create an illusion of movement and depth found in nature.

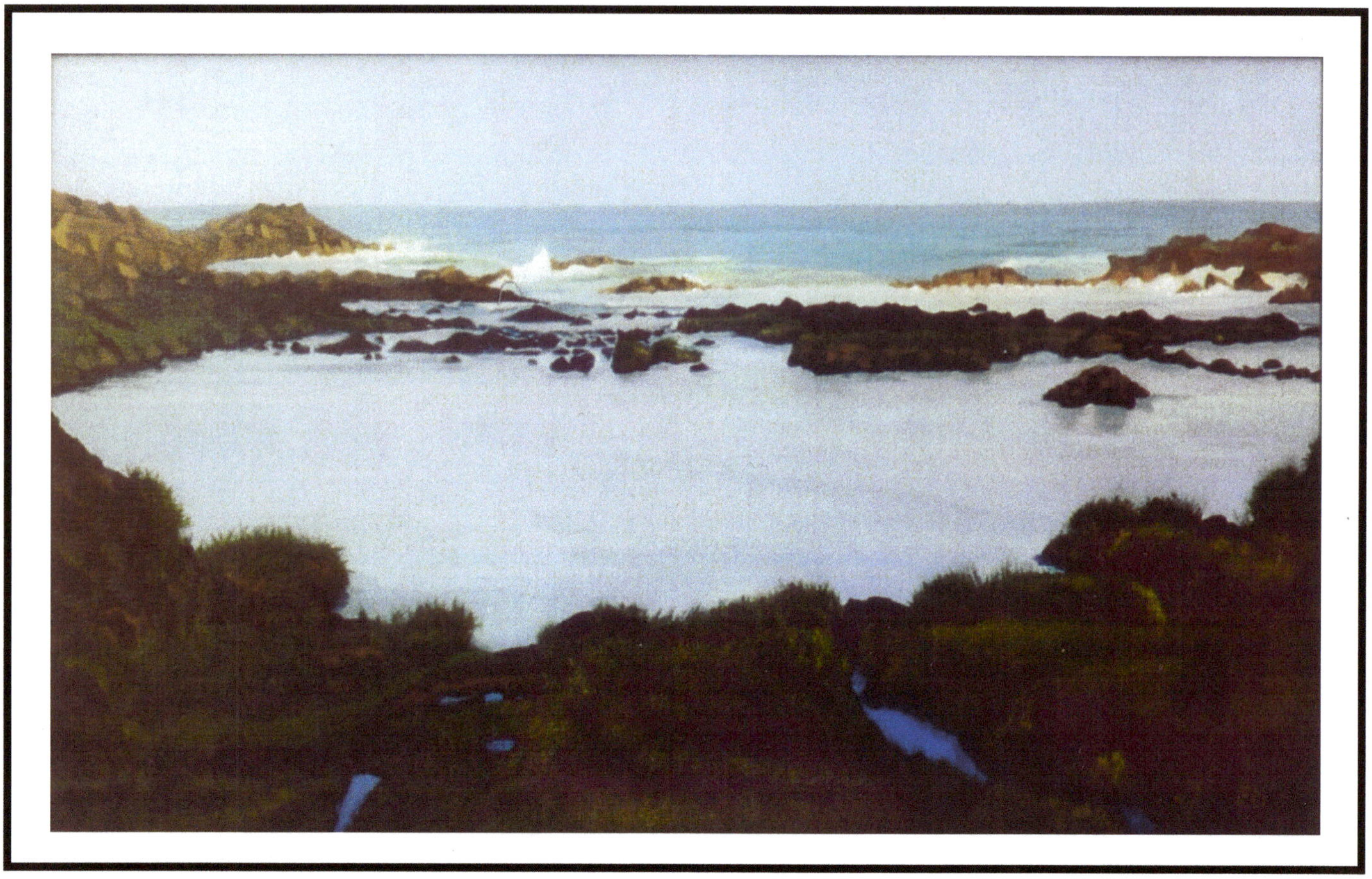

"LALAKEA PONDS"
Oil painting, 18 x 24 inches.   2005.   Private collection.   Mayor's Award, Wailoa Art Center.

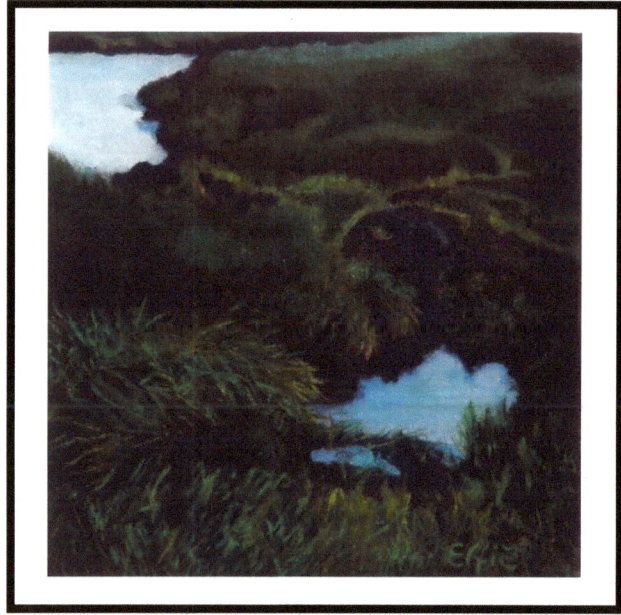

"OCEAN GRASS, I"
Oil painting, 10 x 10 inches.   2002
Private collection.

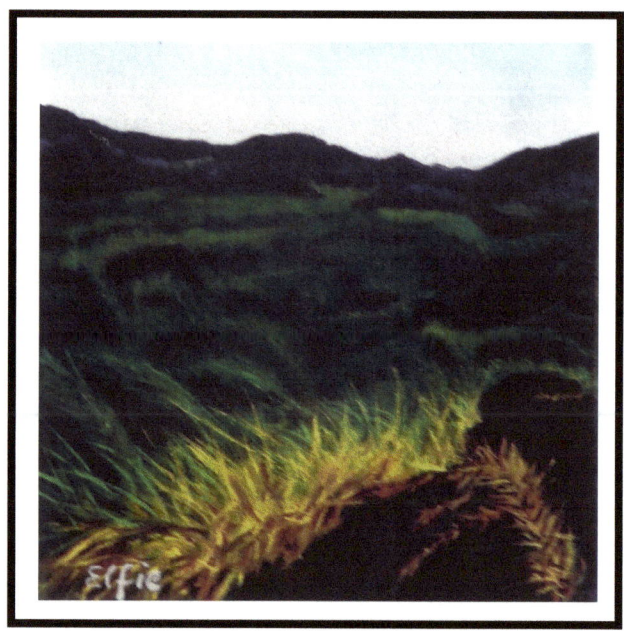

"OCEAN GRASS, II"
Oil painting, 10 x 10 inches.   2002
Private collection.

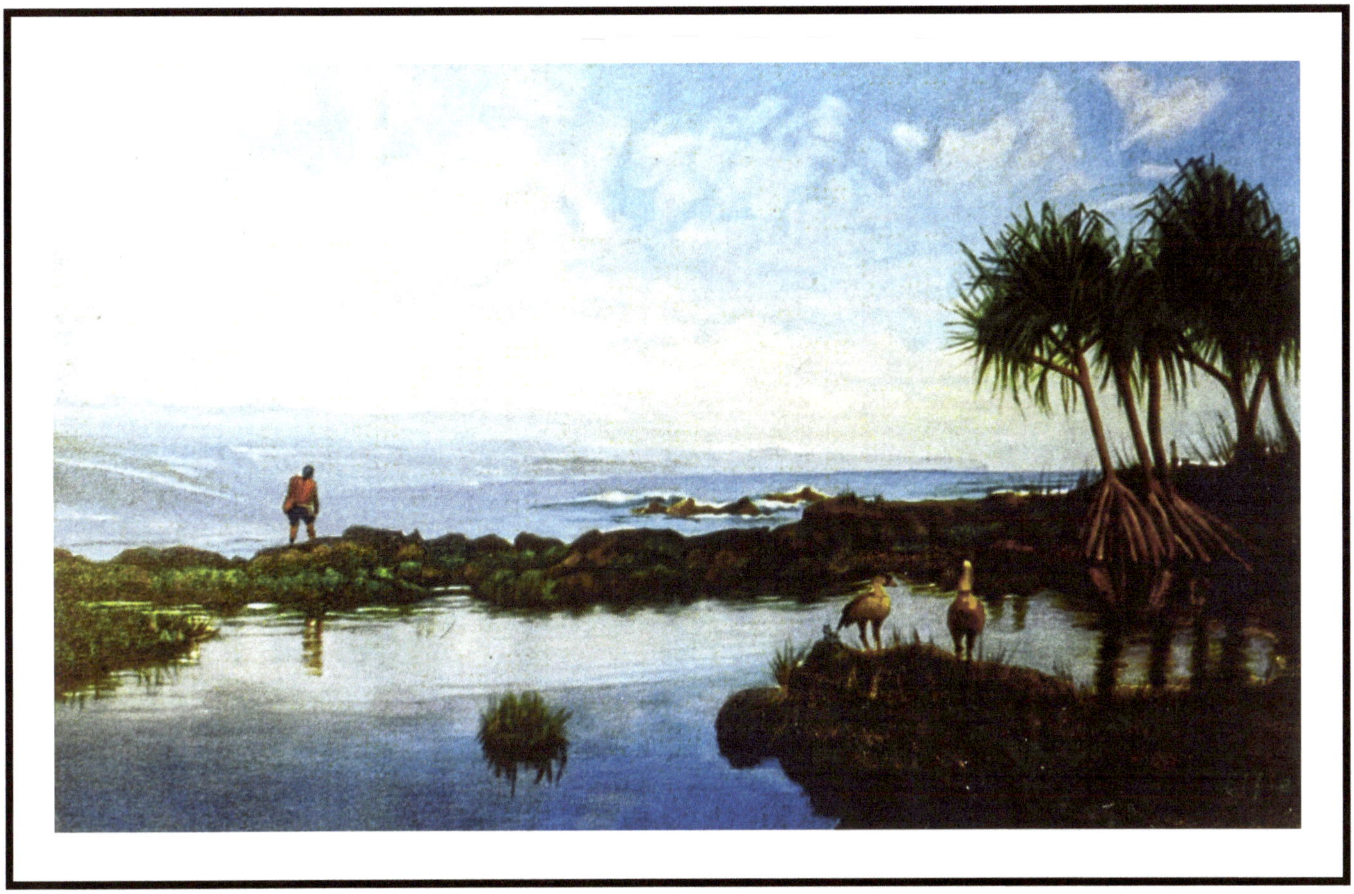

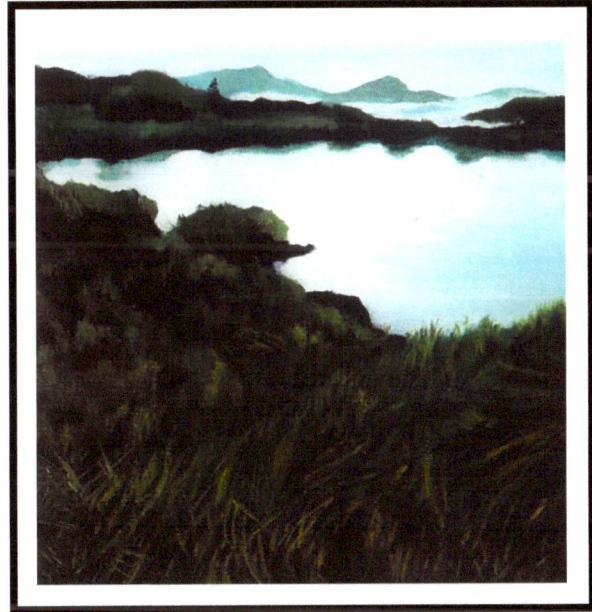

" VISITORS"
Oil painting, 16 x 20 inches.   2003   Collection of the artist. Mayor's Award, Wailoa Art Center.

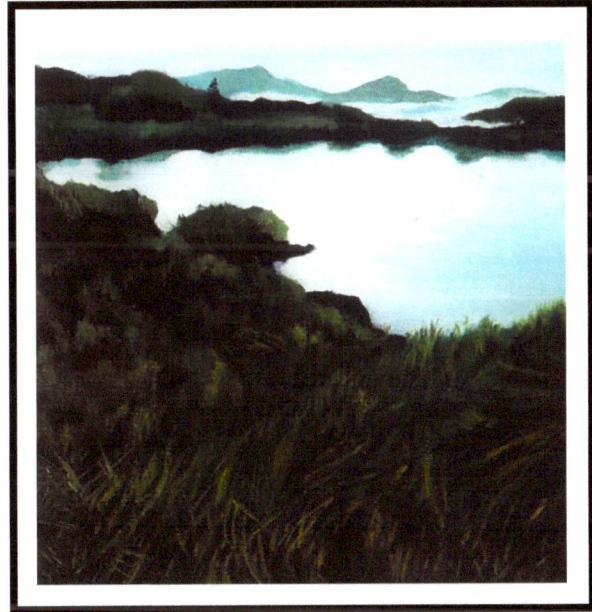

"OCEAN GRASS, III"
Oil painting, 10 x 10 inches   2006
Collection of Margaret Elcock.

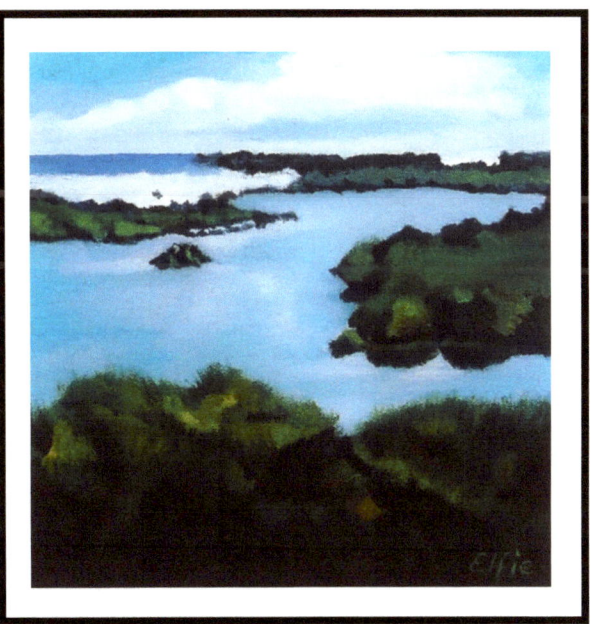

"OCEAN GRASS, IV
Oil painting, 10 x 10 inches.   2006
Collection of Margaret Elcock

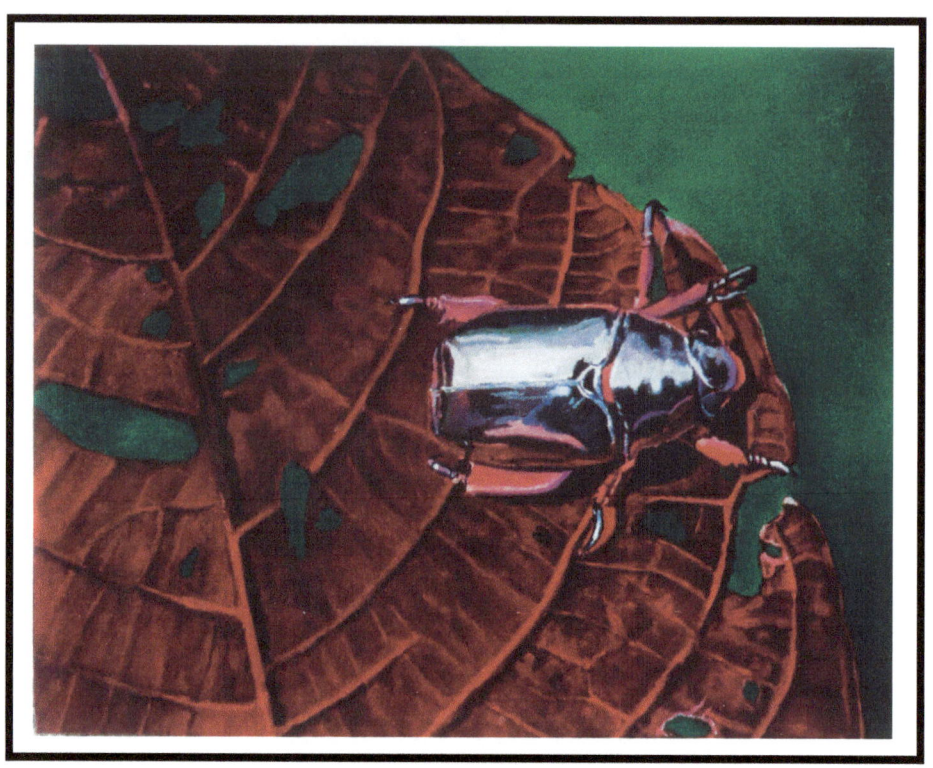

"SILVER SCARAB"
Oil painting, 11 x 14 inches.   2003
Collection of Mr. and Mrs. Bedford

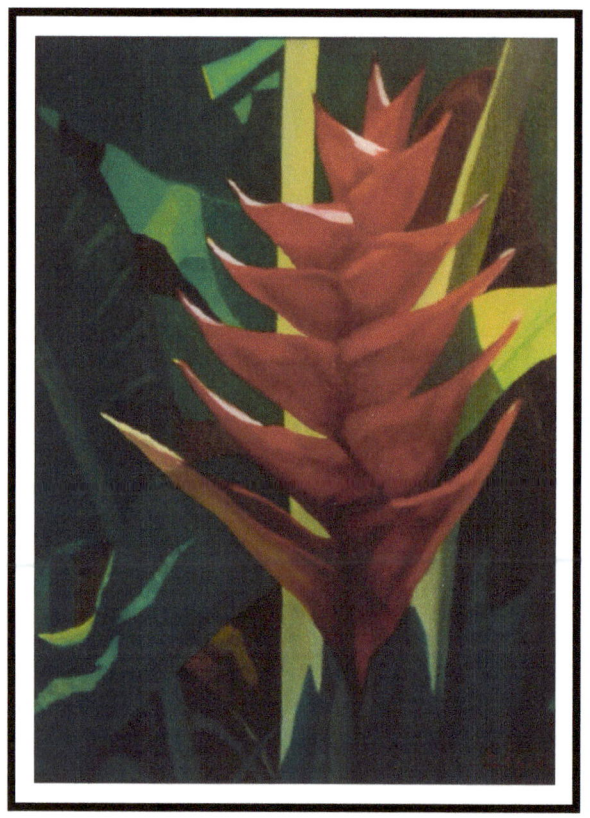

"HELICONIA"
Oil painting, 16 X 20 inches.   2005
Collection of Lena Higa

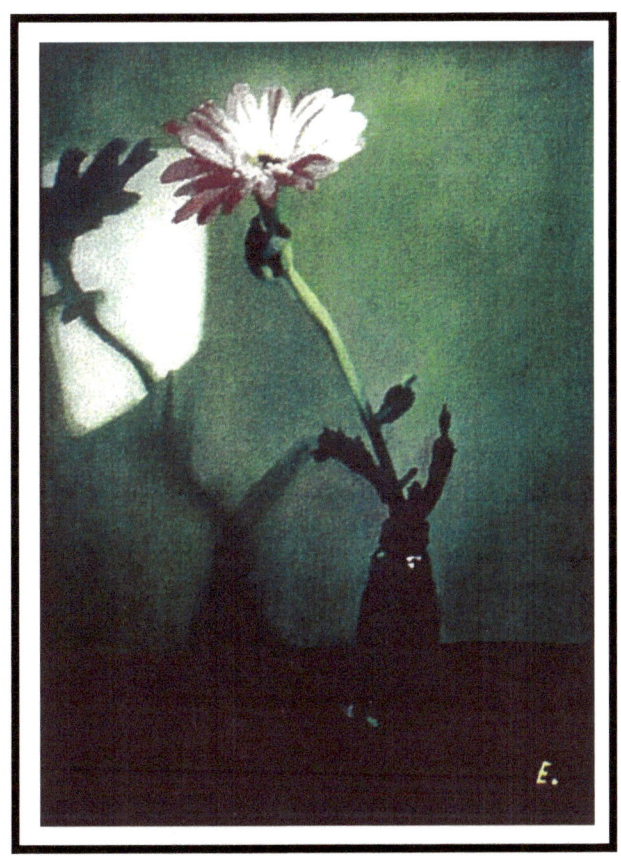

"GERBERA"
Oil painting, 12 x 9 inches.   2004
Collection of Laura McDonald & Hope Northway

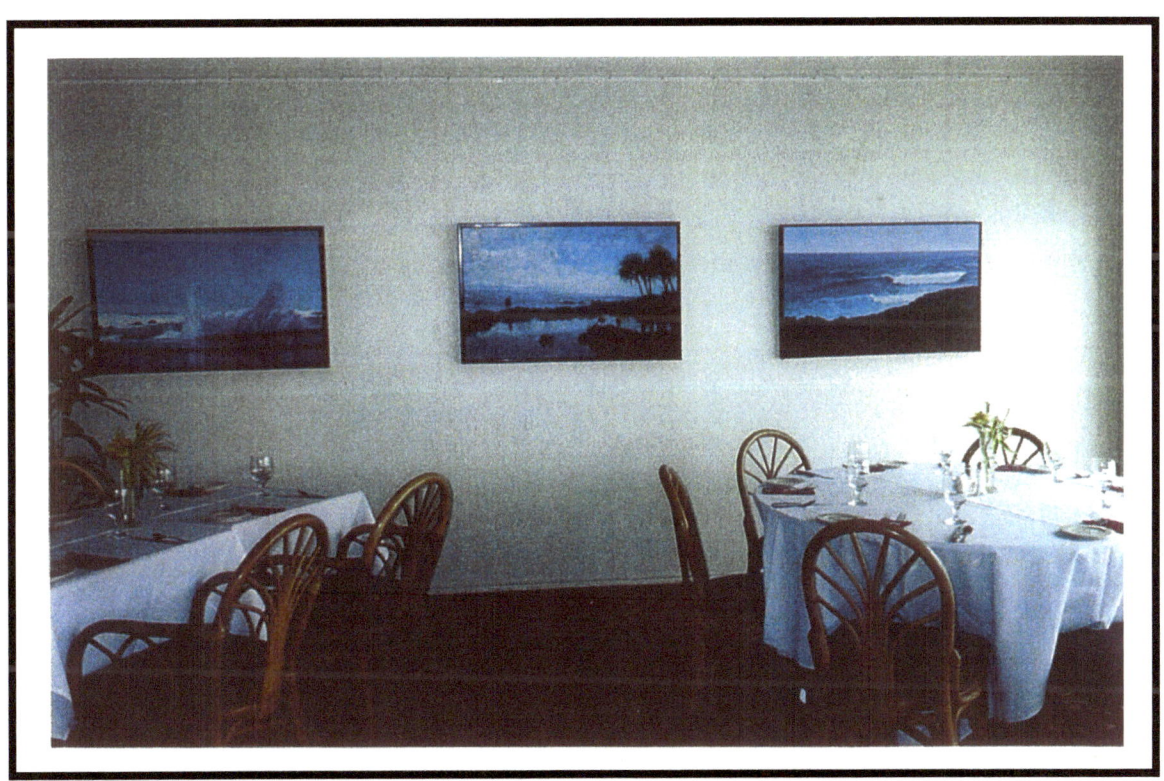

Landscape and floral paintings on display at the Hilo Yacht Club

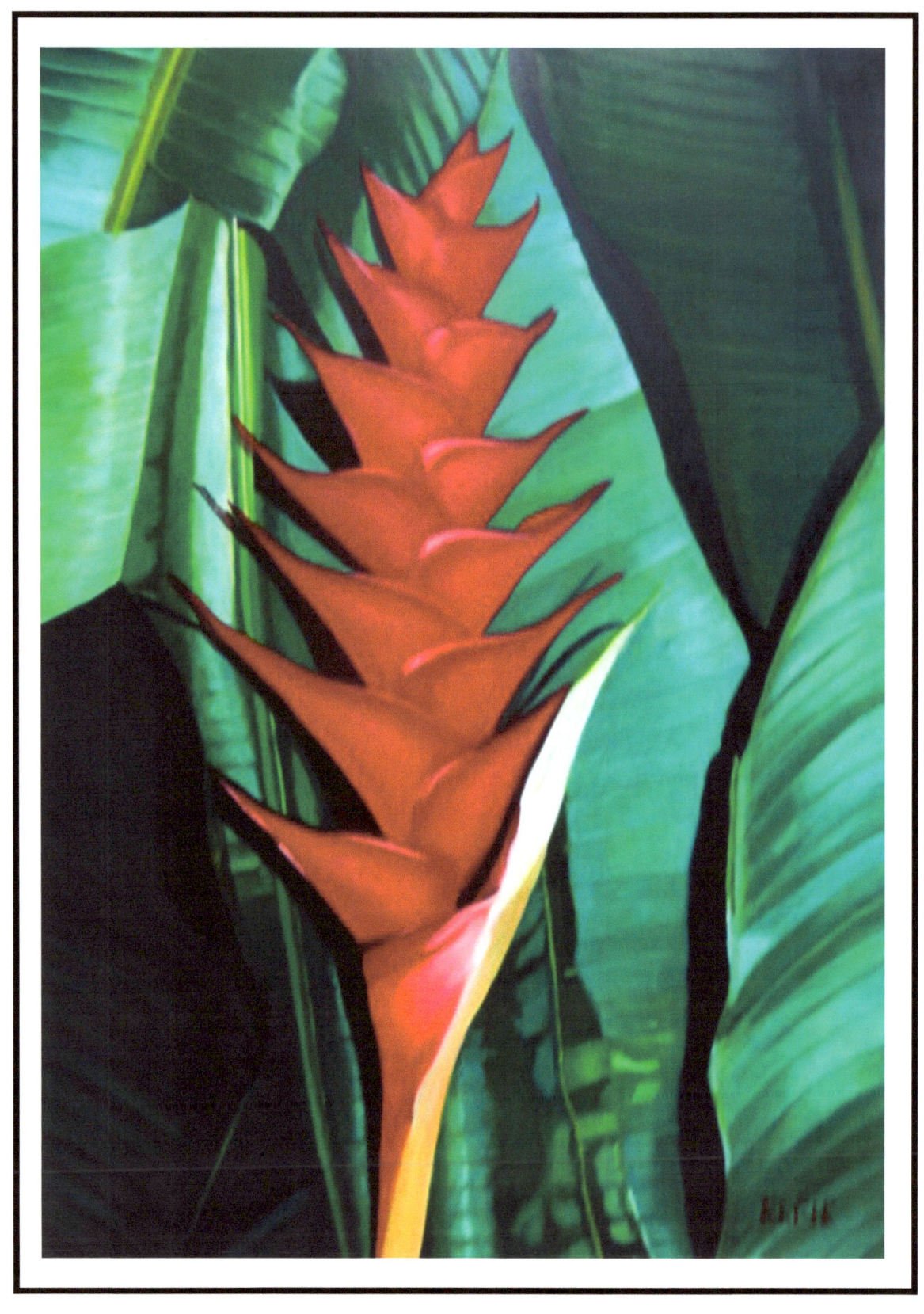

"RED HELICONIA"
Oil painting. 40 X 30 inches. 2005
Collection of EHCC/Hawai'i Museum of Contemporary Art

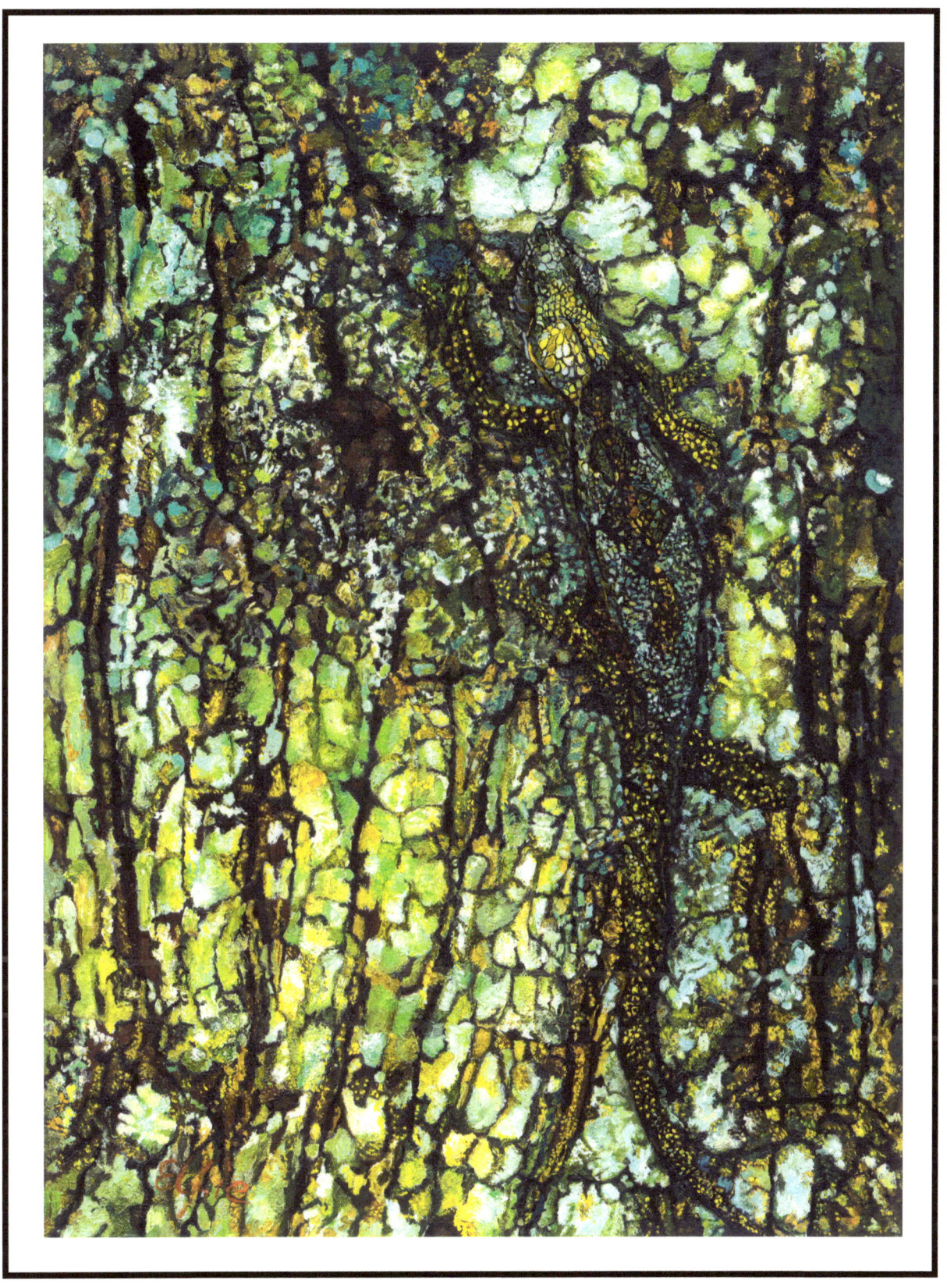

"NOW YOU SEE IT NOW YOU DON'T"
Oil painting, 18 x 14 inches.   1999
Private collection

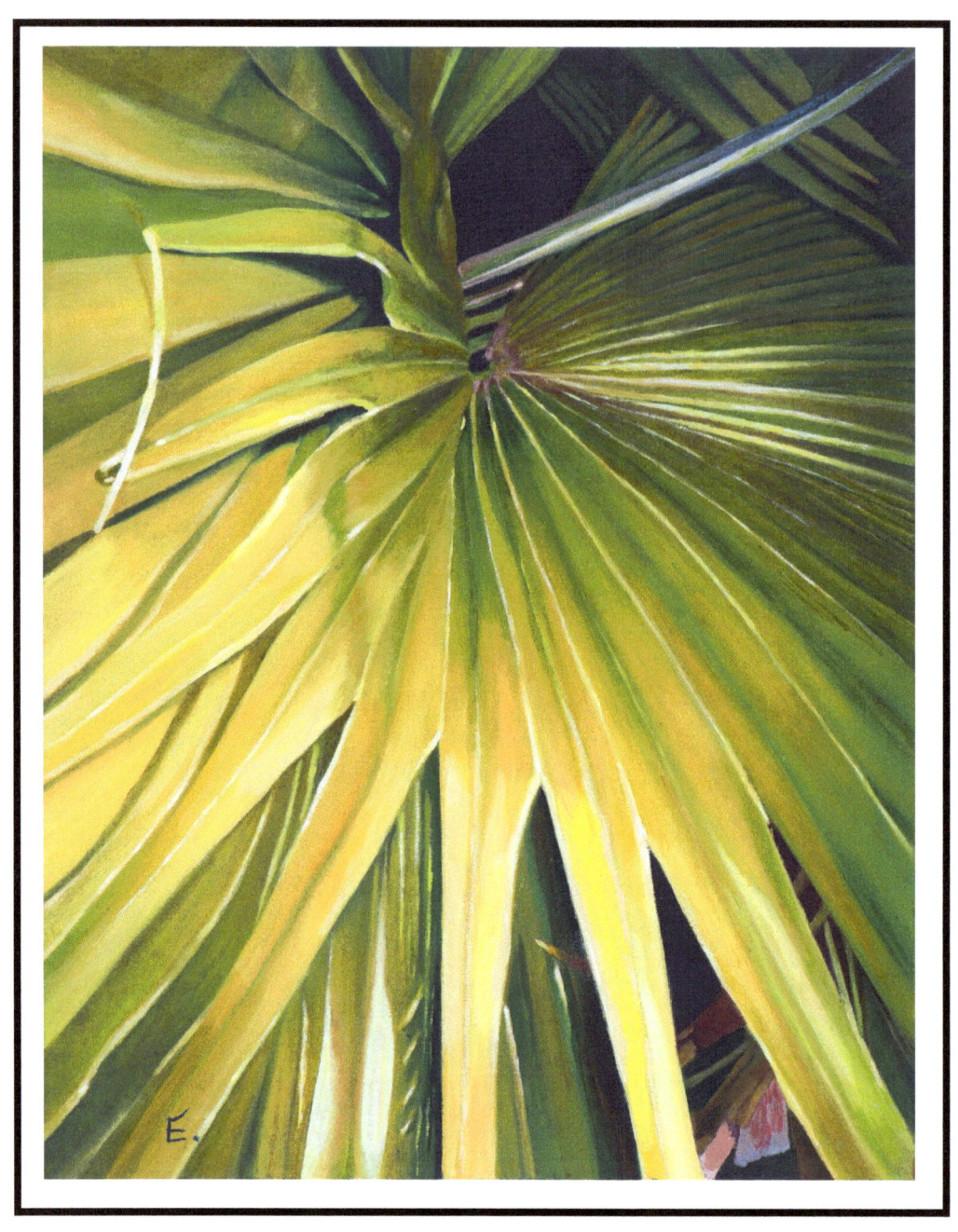

"HALENA"
Oil painting, 18 x 14 inches.   2001
Collection of Mr. & Mrs. Sebala

This was the first palm I ever painted. The pattern on the frond, the delicate coloring and the unusual view from above was too enticing for me not to photograph it. I found this yellow palm, Halena, at the entrance of the Hilo zoo. It was a young palm since I was able to look down inside of it while photographing it. I enjoy experimenting therefore decided to try a new technique called "grisaille." It is a monochromatic value painting often done in black and white. The advantage of this technique is that the entire value system within the painting has been accomplished as an under-painting allowing the painter to be only concerned with the application of colors on top of the "grisaille," Basically the method is a two layer technique; first the lights and darks are applied, then the colors. After this first palm frond painting I began to paint many more palms.

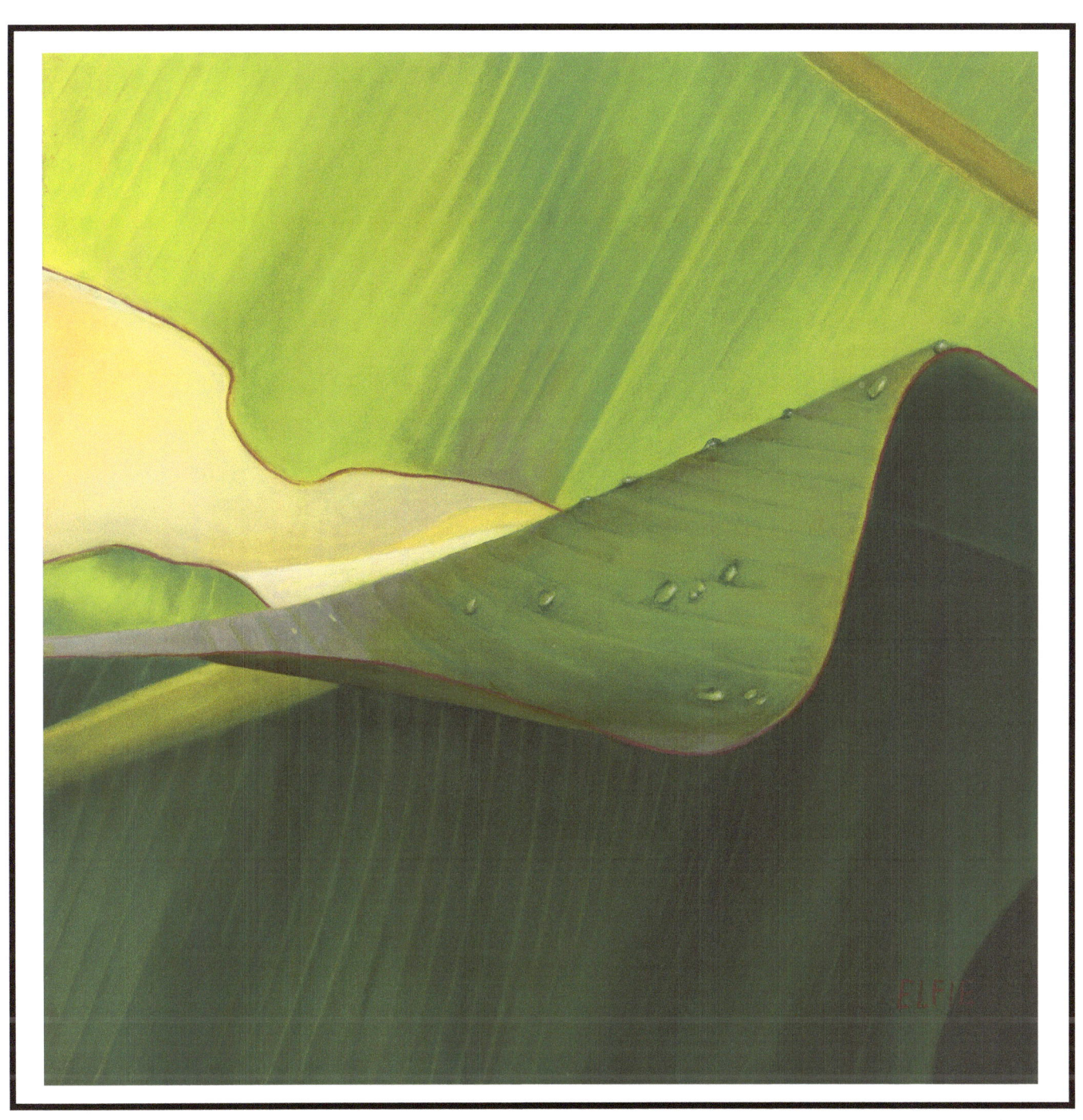

"WAVE"
Oil painting, 24 x 24 inches.   2014
Collection of Lourdan Kimbrell

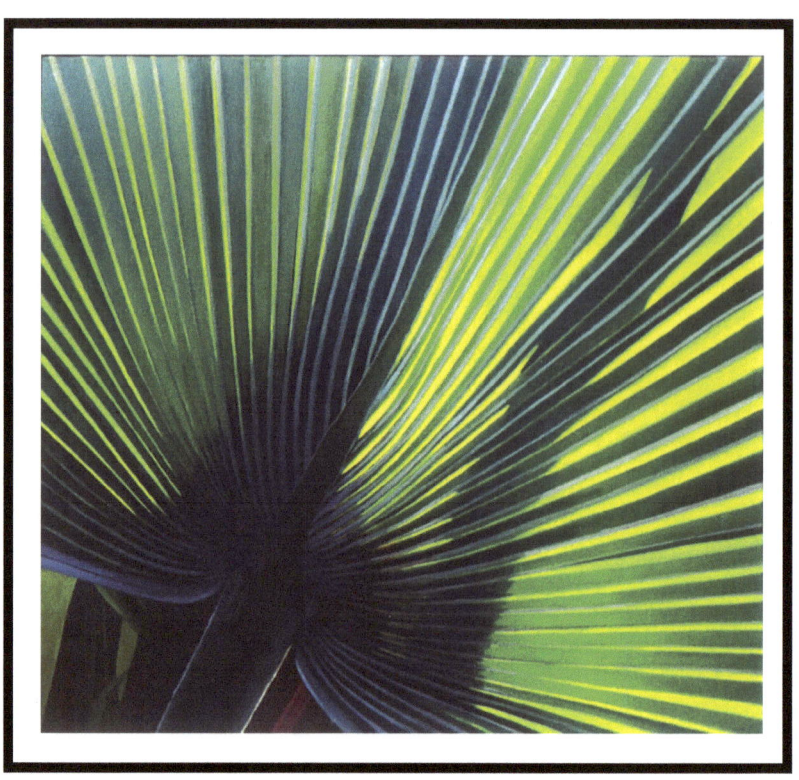

"TWIN PALM I"
Oil painting, 32 x 40 inches.   2004
Private collection

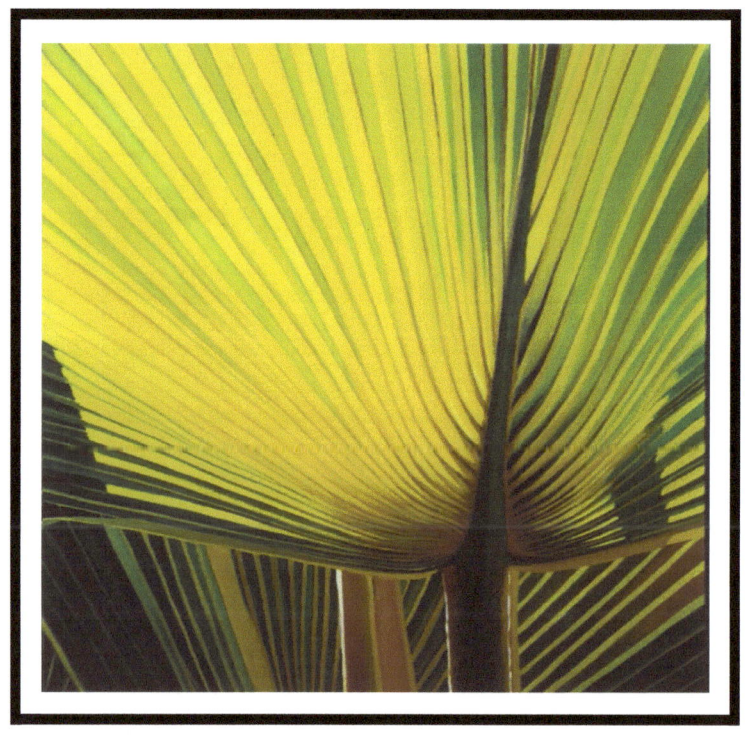

"FAN PALM"
Oil painting, 36 x 32 inches   2004
Private collection

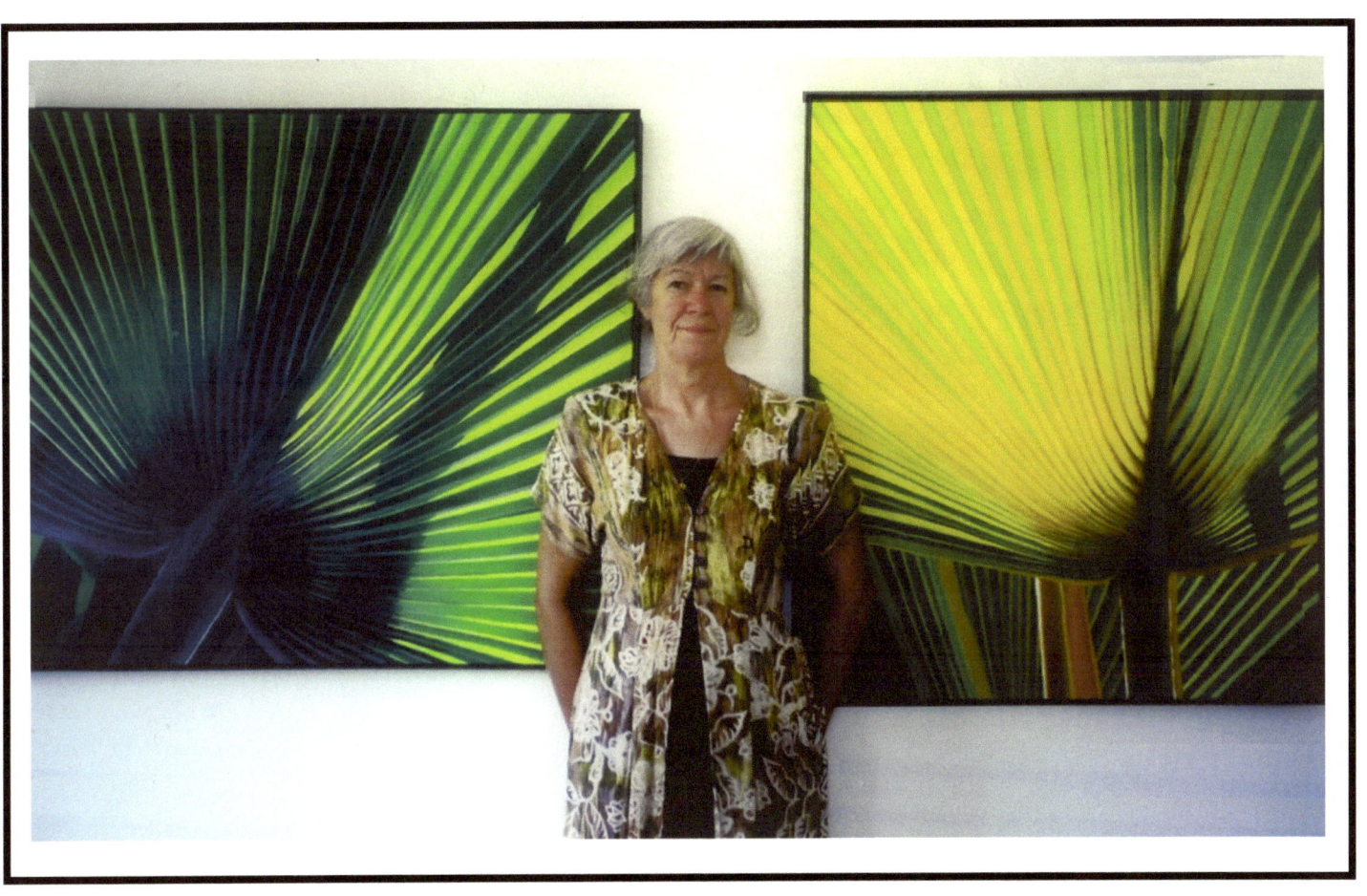

In front of 'Twin Palm' and 'Twin Palm I' at the opening of the exhibition "In the Garden" at the Hawaii Museum of Contemporary Art in 2004. This photo shows the scale of the paintings. I prefer to work large scale as it offers me the opportunity to develop the quality of light of the subject matter.

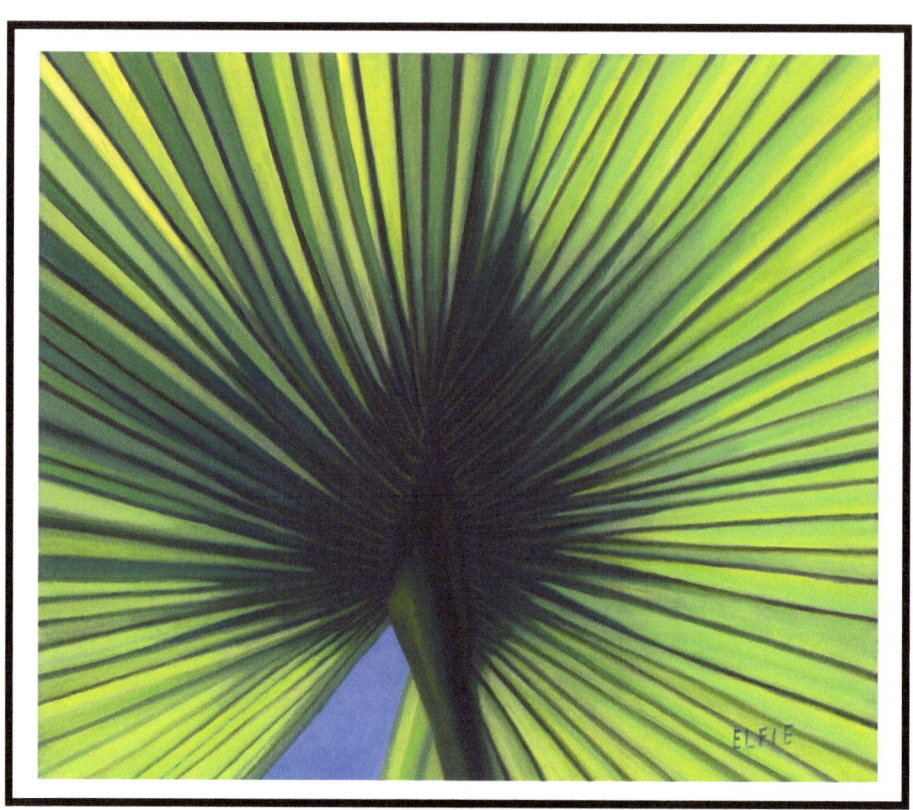

"FAN PALM VII"
Oil painting, 36 X 42 inches.   2004
Collection of the artist

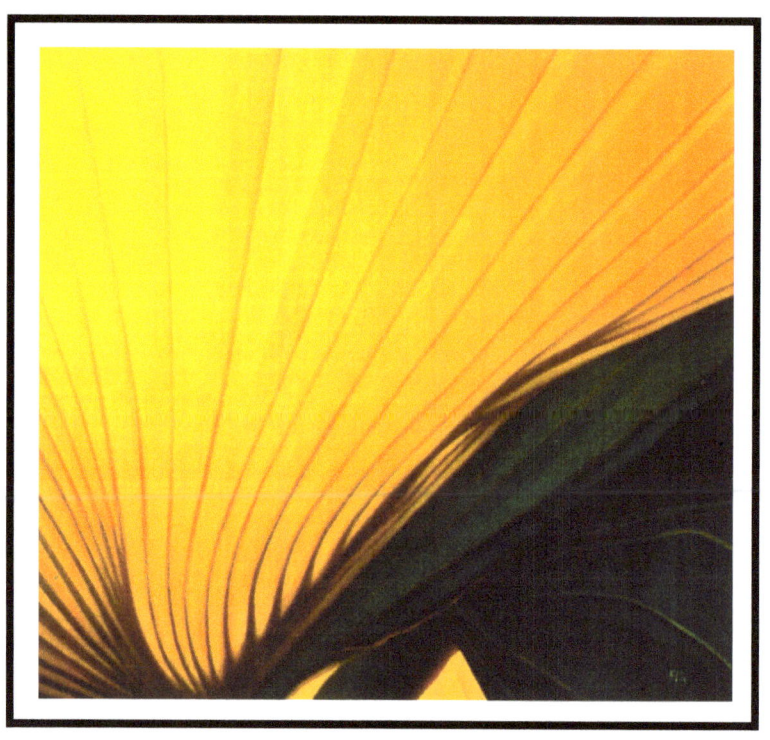

"FAN PALM"
Oil painting, 36 x 32 inches   2004
Private collection

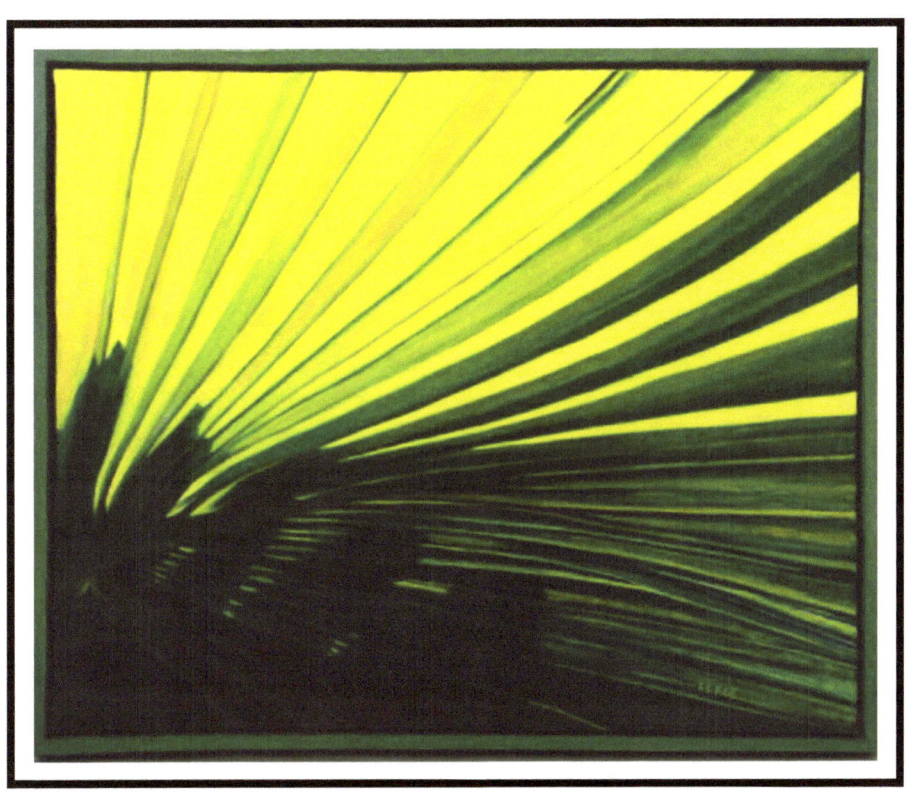

"VARIEGATED PALM"
Oil painting, 36 x 48 inches   2005
Private Collection

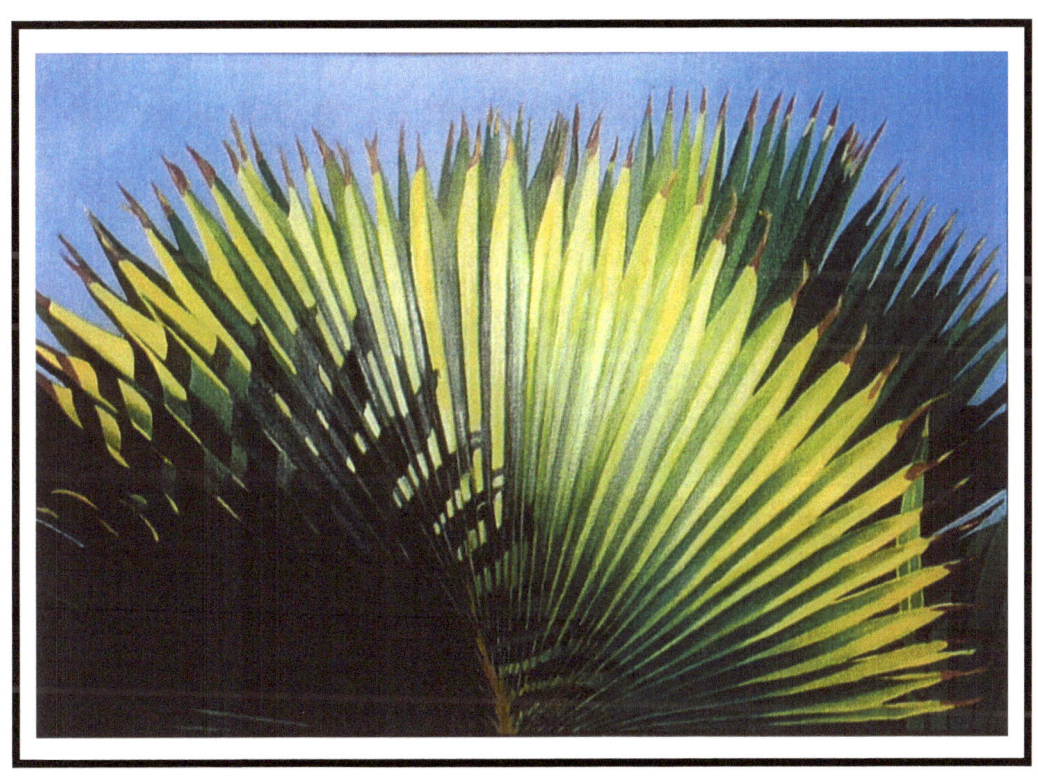

"NATURE'S FAN"
Oil painting, 36 x 42 inches   2004
Private collection

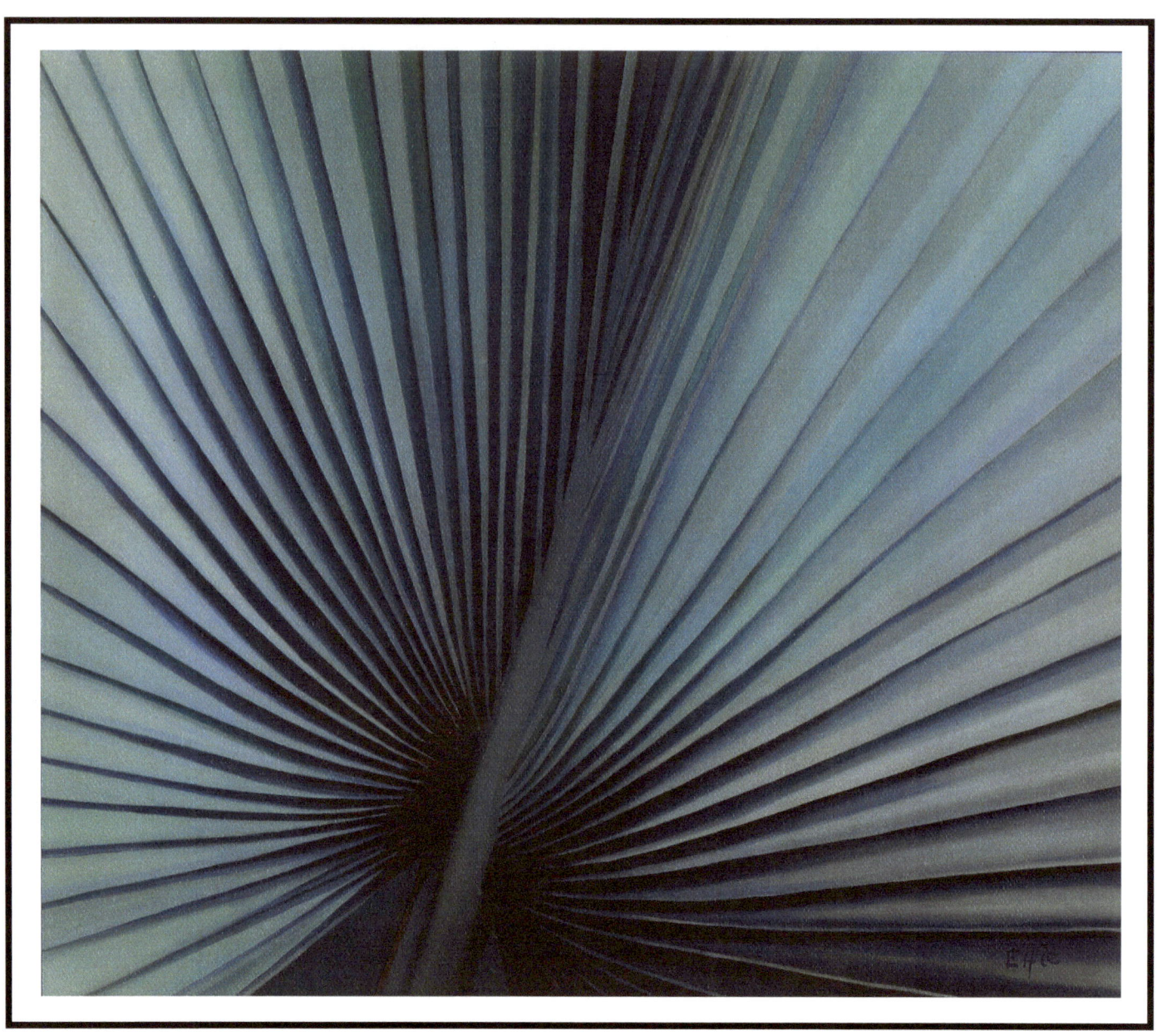

"BLUE LATAN"
Oil painting, 36 x 42 inches.   2007,
Collection of Patrick Edwards

Mr. Edwards told me the reasons why he wanted this particular work was because of the bluish color and the large size of the canvas so he bought this painting. He placed "Blue Latan" over a couch on a center wall of his living room. If anyone wishes to see the size of the original work they can visit the Hilo Hospice where a Giclee print hangs on the wall.

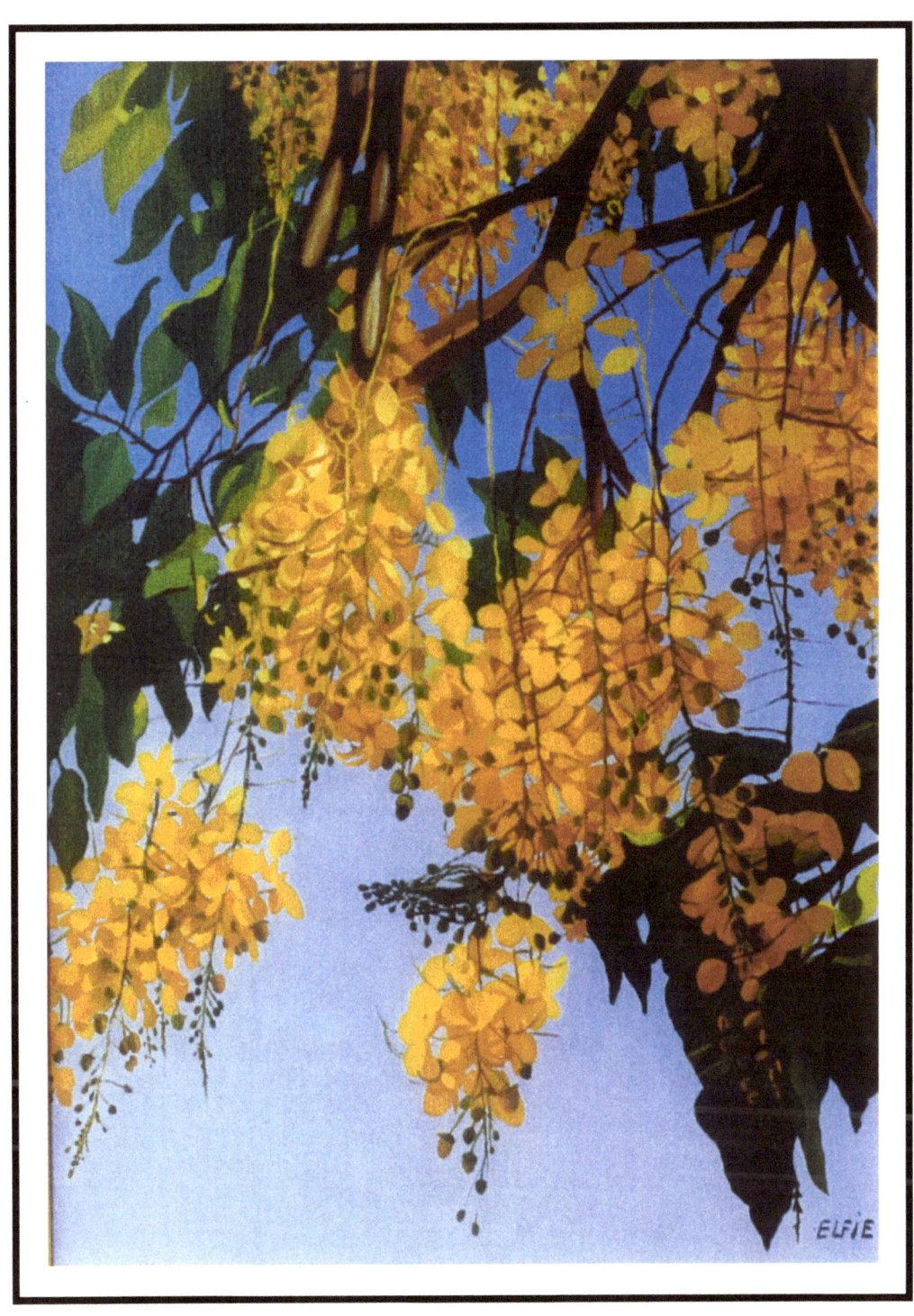

"YELLOW SHOWER",
Oil painting, 34 x 24 inches.   2003
Collection of Vickie Vierra

Every year around May I would see this Shower Tree at the Kawamoto Pool where I swim. I found the color and the delicate small blossoms with grape-like patterns irresistible. "One day," I thought, "I have to paint those flowers." At the time I took the photo of the blossoms there was a light wind blowing the branches gently sideways. I made certain while painting the scene that the movement of the wind would be visible, at least to me.

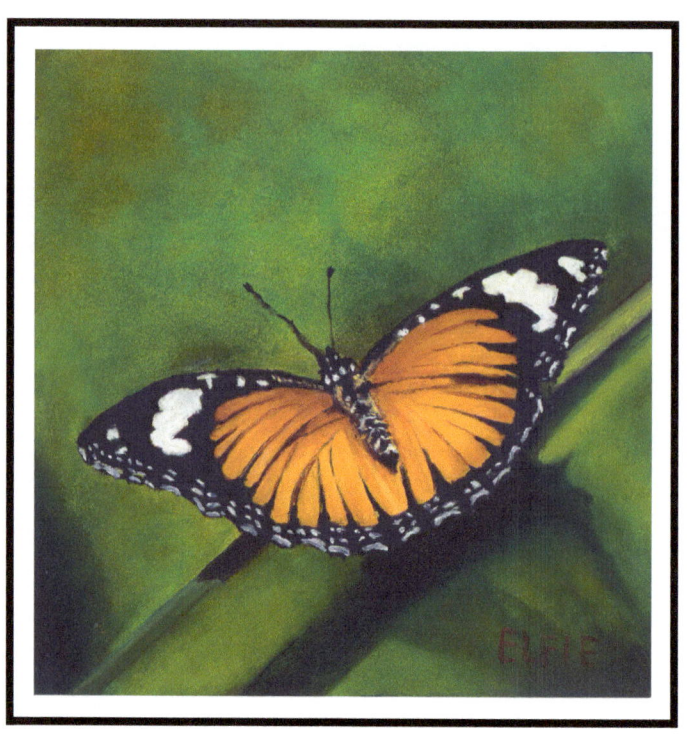

"BUTTERFLY"
Oil painting, 8 x 8 inches. 2014
Collection of Kelly Hudson

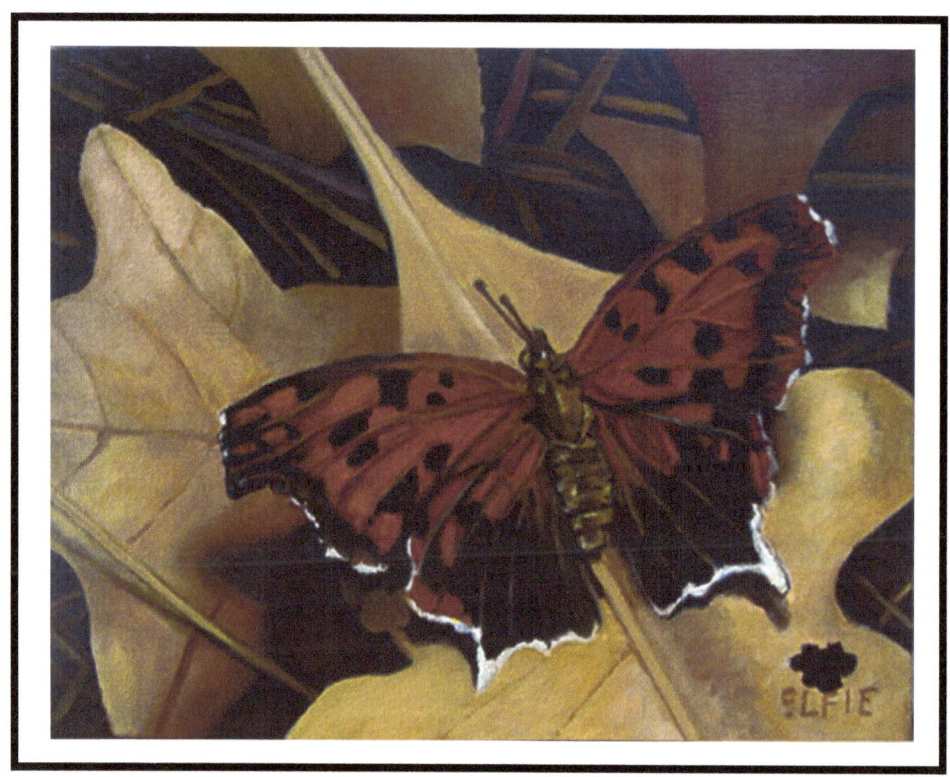

"BUTTERFLY"
Oil painting, 9 x 12 inches. 2014
Private collection

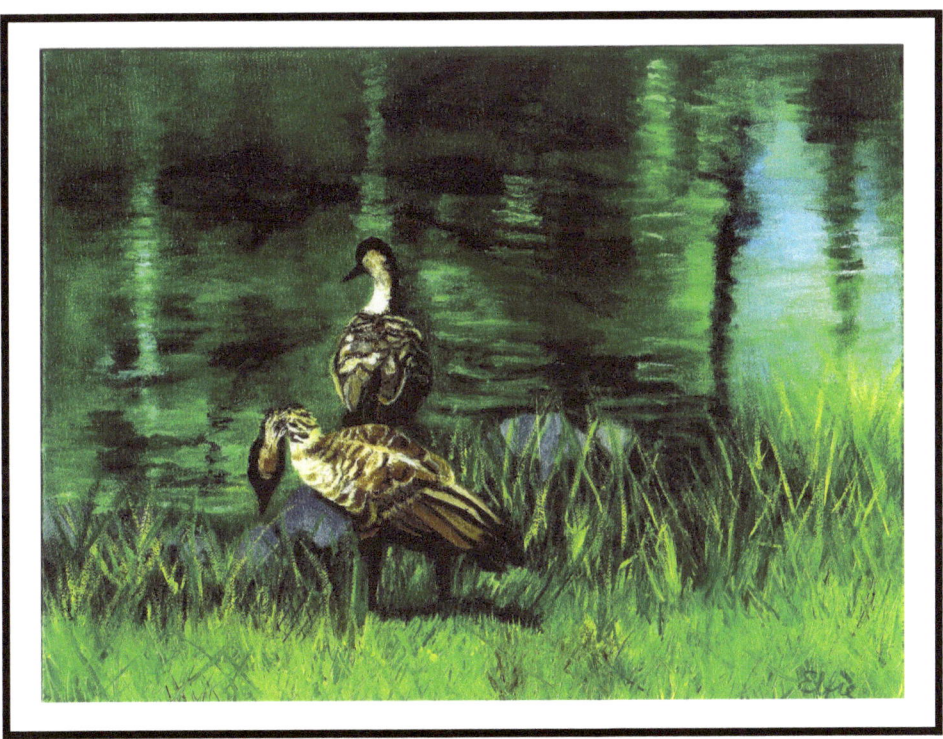

"NENE AT RICHARDSON BEACH"
Oil painting, 11 x 14 inches.   1999

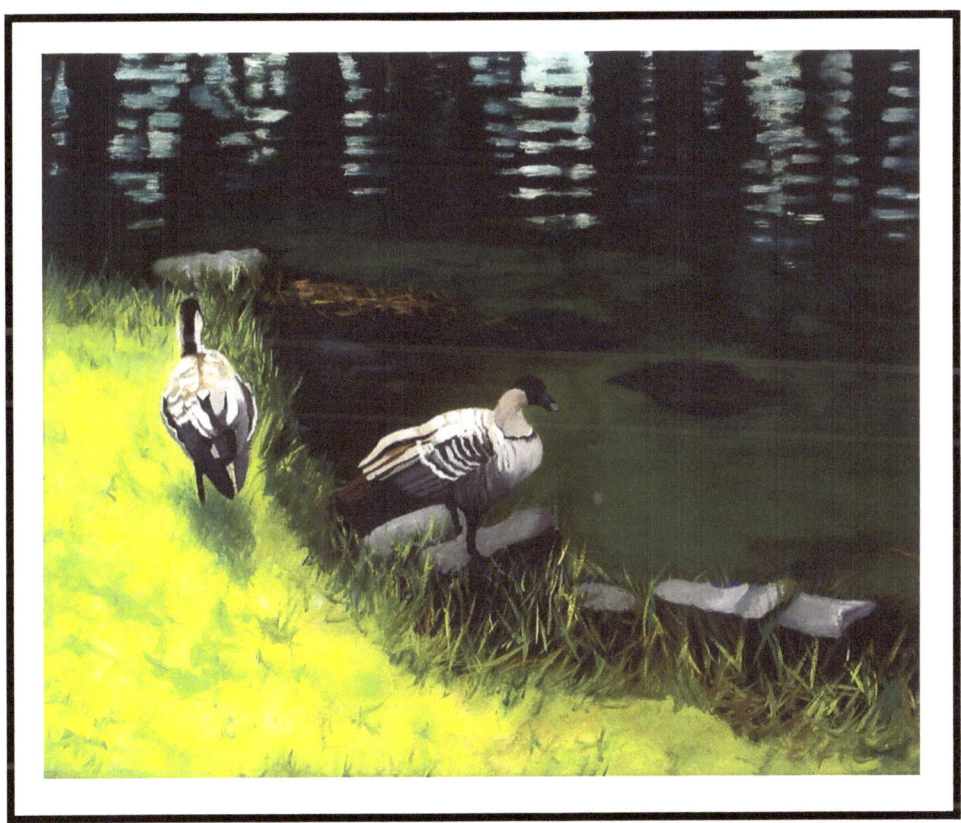

"NENE AT WAIOLENA"
Oil painting, 34 X 40 inches.   1998
Private collection

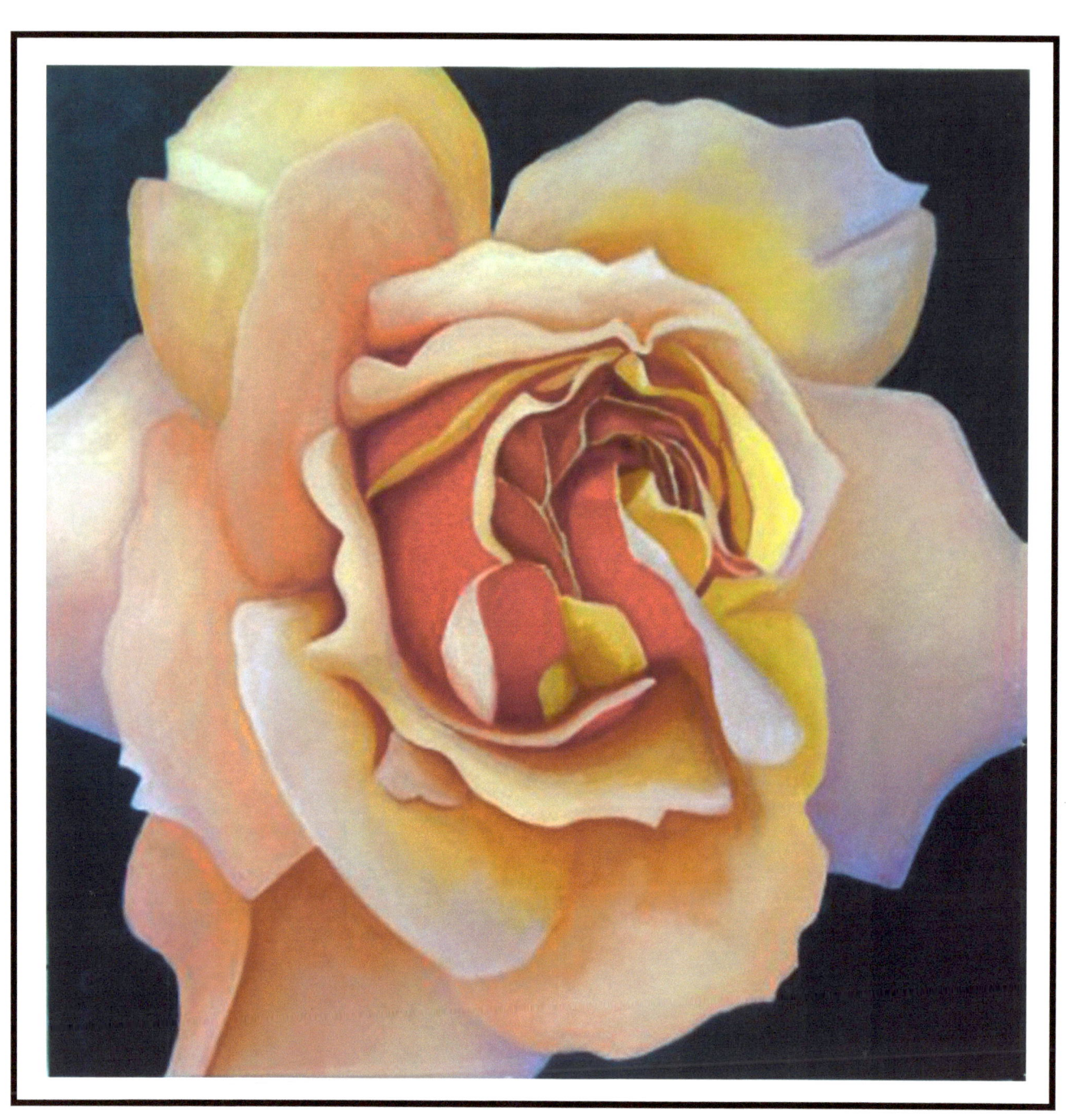

"ROSE"
Oil painting, 24 x 24 inches,   2010

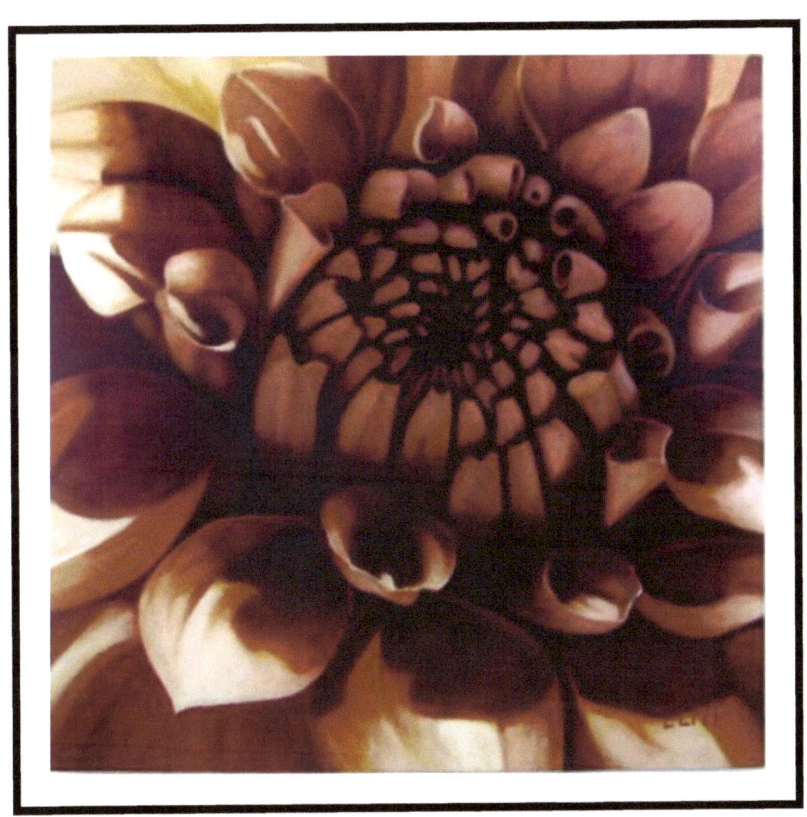

"DAHLIA"
Oil painting, 24 x 24 inches, 2012

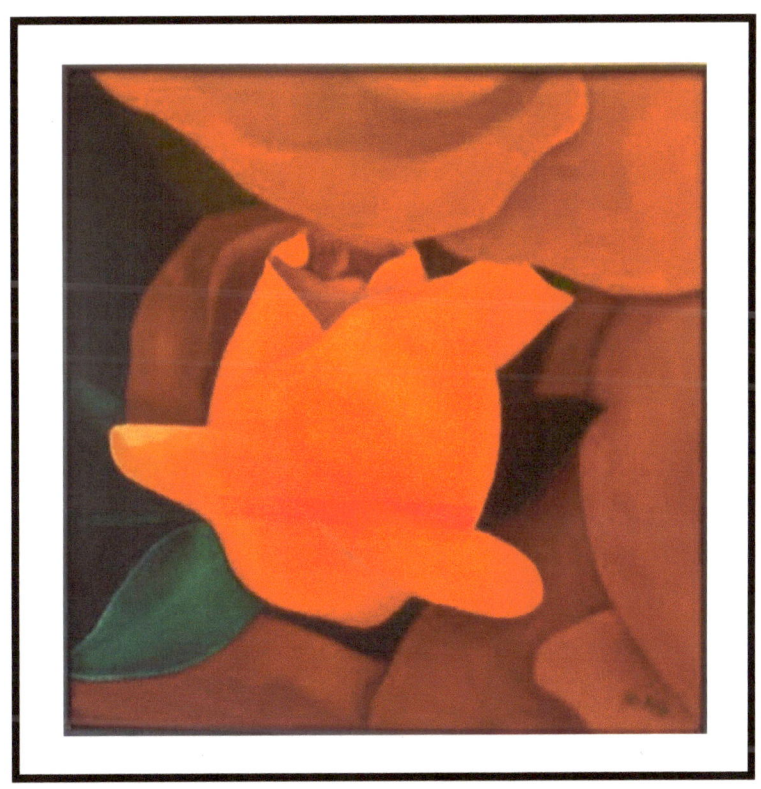

"ROSEBUD"
Oil painting, 20 x 20 inches. 2010
Private collection

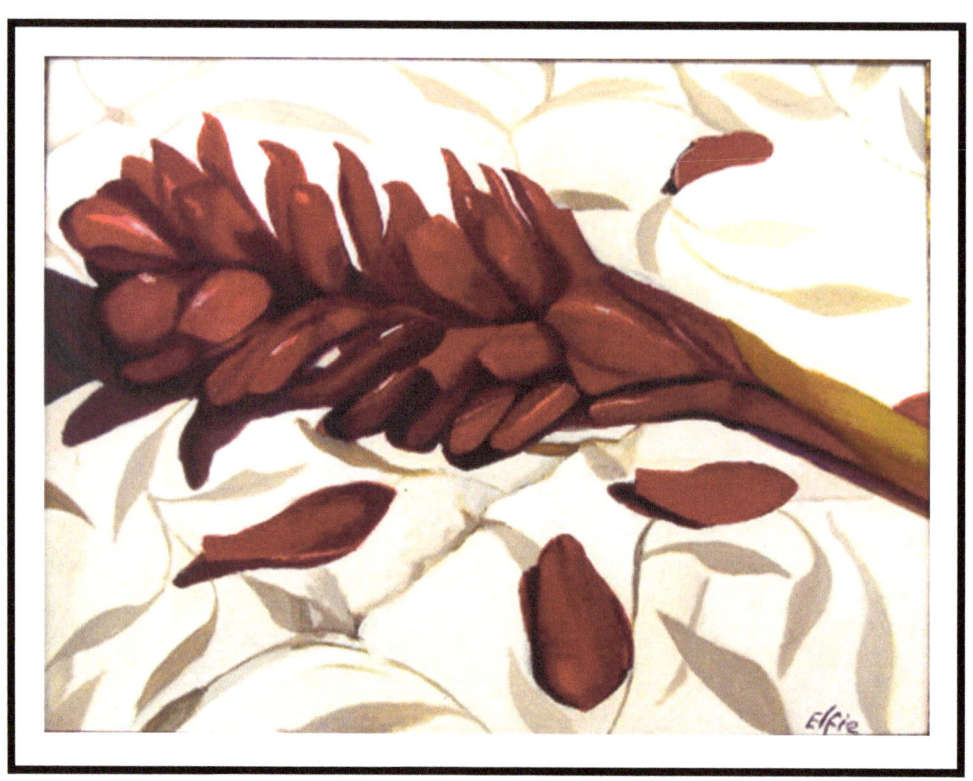

"RED GINGER"
Oil painting, 11 X 14 inches.   2003
Collection of EHCC/Hawaii Museum of Contemporary Art

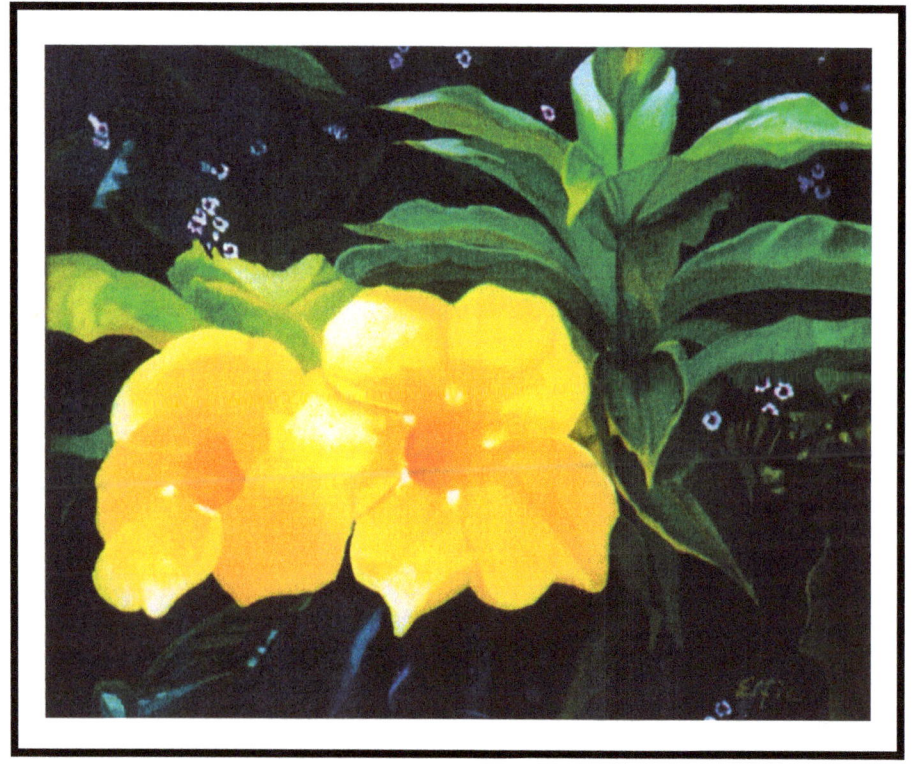

"THE COUPLE"
Oil painting , 16 x 20 inches.   2007
Collection of Mr. & Mrs. Petrovic

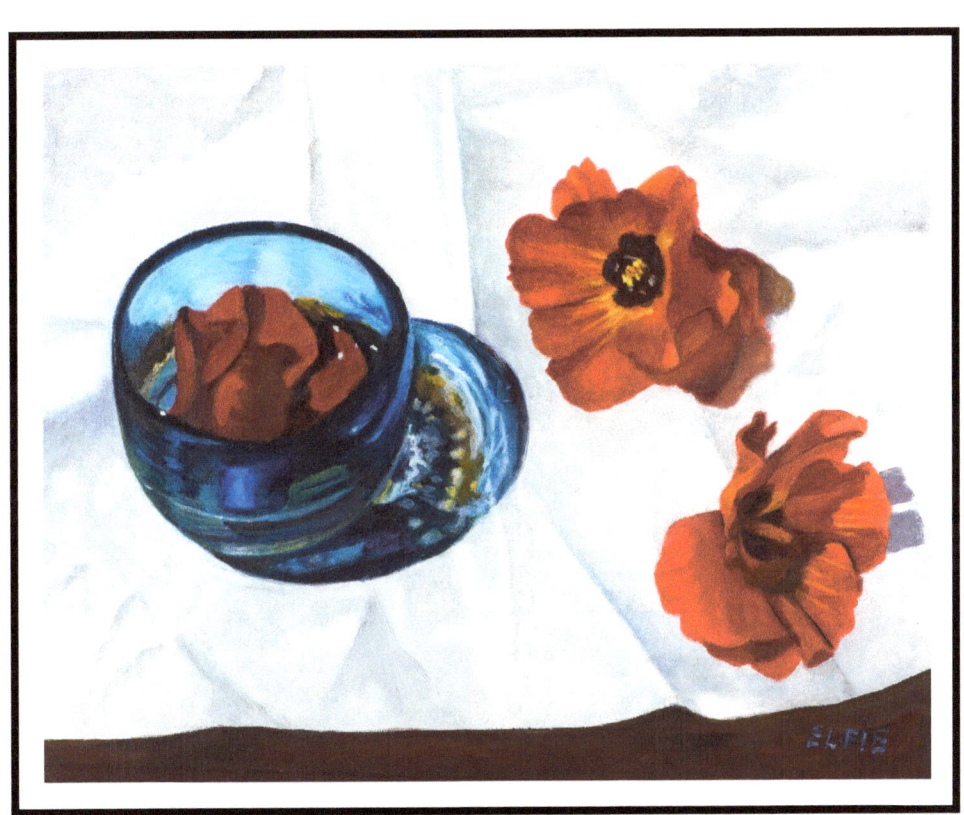

"HAU"
Oil painting, 16 x 20 inches.   2013

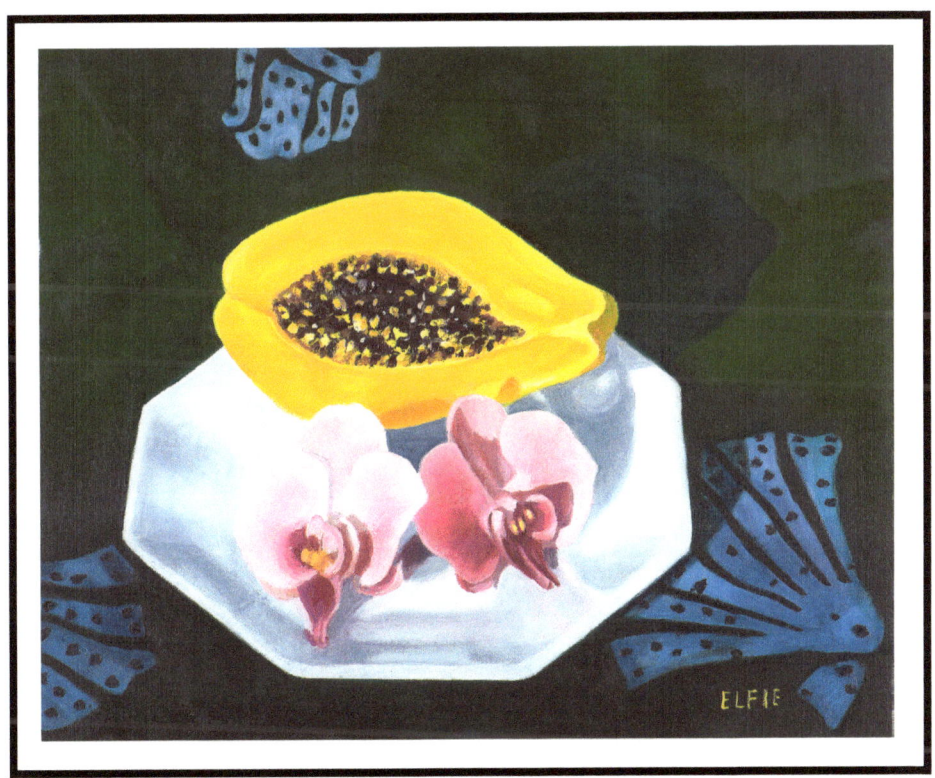

"PAPAYA"
Oil painting, 18 X 14 Inches.   2013
Private collection

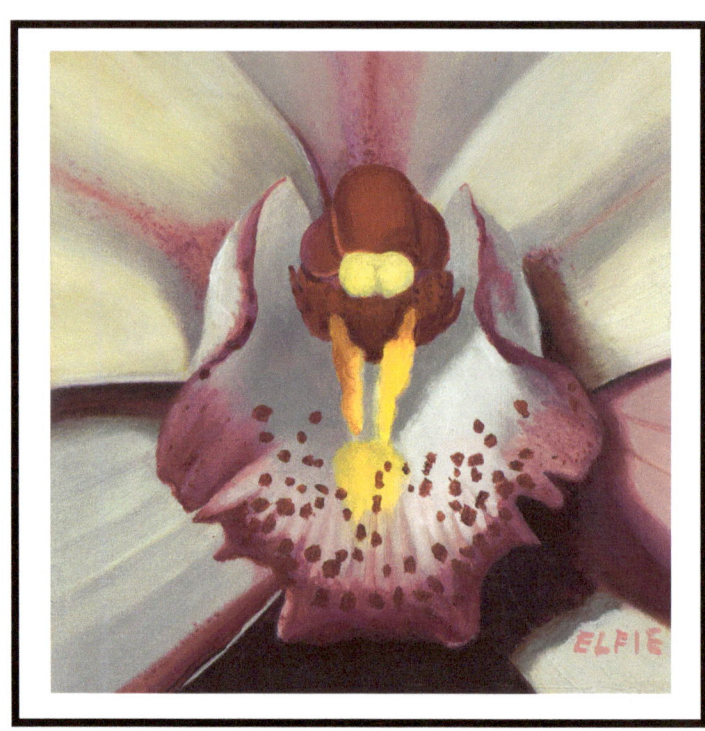

"ORCHID WITH SPOTS"
Oil painting, 8 X 8 inches.   2013
Private collection

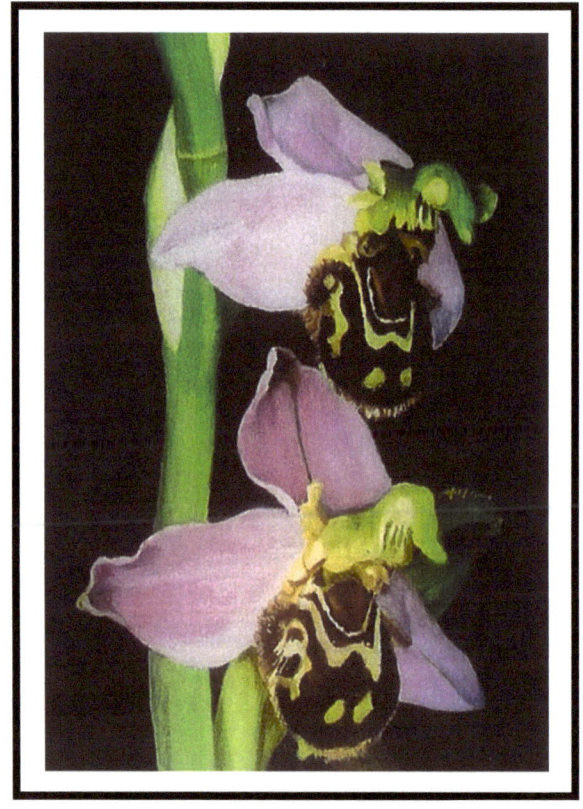

"WILD ORCHID"
Oil painting, 12 X 9 inches.   2014
Private collection

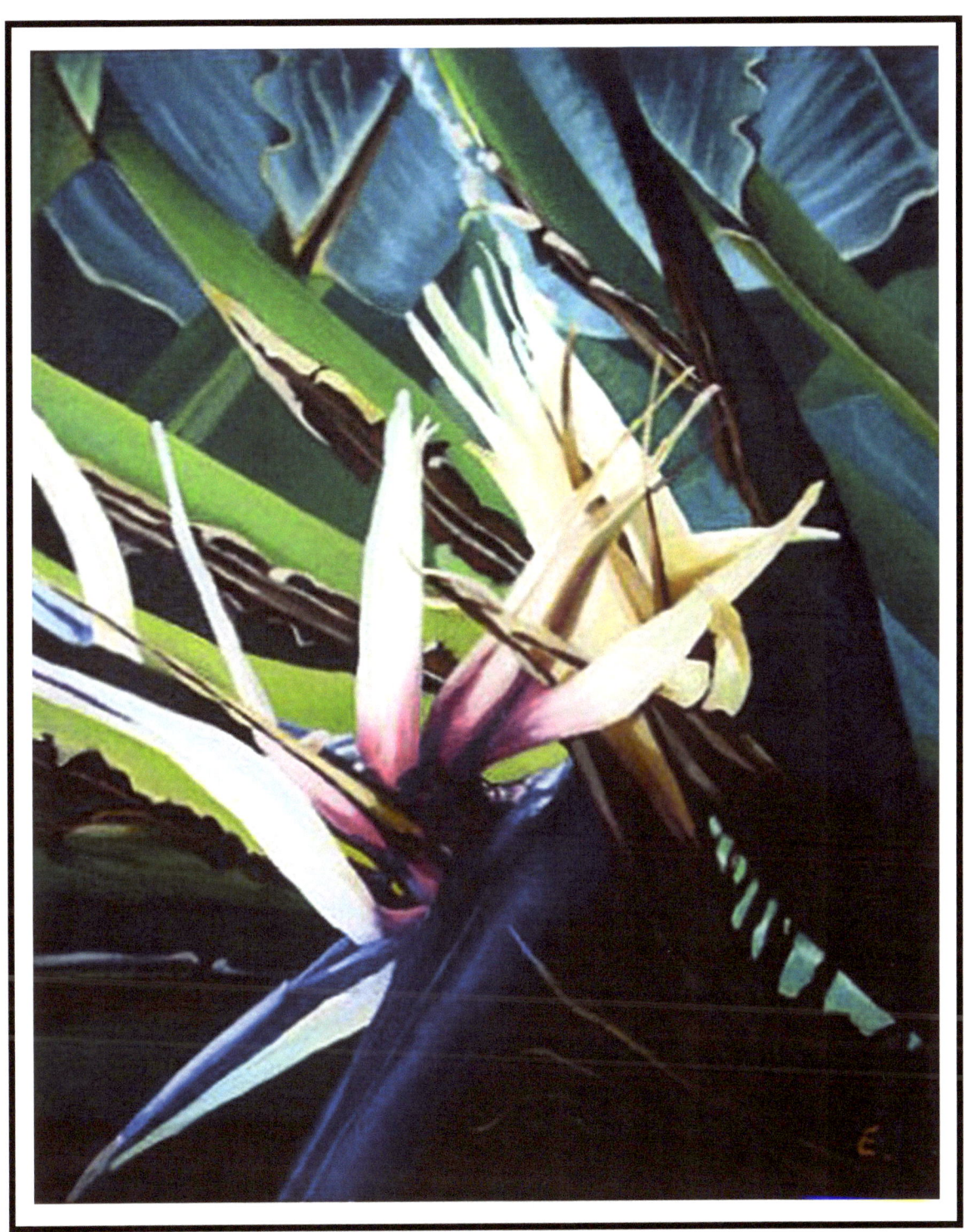

"ENCOUNTER"
Oil painting, 20 x 16 inches.   1998
Private collection

PEOPLE TO THANK

The individual who has received my profound thanks is my husband, Robert. He encouraged me to take UCLA Extension art classes and go back to school even though I was already a mother.

I wish to thank all of the students who have taken my classes; children, inmates, adults and seniors. They motivate me to keep current about new teaching methods, media and contemporary art.

A special thank you to my good friends, Lena and Ruth.
There are many other people that I wish to thank: colleagues, friends, art collectors and all the others who enhance my life by encouraging me to be true to myself.

Rose Adare
Alyce Arata
Annie Bedford
Henry Bianchini
Marie Burns
Tom and Maryanne Downey
Paul Edwards
Margueite Elcock
Dr. Mary Graner
Gretchen Grove
Judy Hara
Ms. K. Hudson
Dr. Houser
Lyn How
David Hubbard
Arthur Johnsen

Claire Kaneshiro
Cody King
Dr. Shapiro & Dr. Rhan Kim
Laura McDonnell
Dr. McGuffy
Alan McNarie
Hope Northway
Mr. & Mrs. Petrovic
Rick and Debbie Ricker
Jim. Rhodes
Ruth and Froilen Rivera
John Ross
Paul Sebala
Donna Saiki
Bruce Sakamoto
Vicki Vierra
Barbara Willams

A special thanks to Randy Takaki for allowing me to finish one of his "Guardians". It was such a fun and joyful experience.

A heartfelt thanks to Lourdan Kimbrell for appreciating all of my artworks even the most unorthodox firmly suggesting that it was time for me to have a retrospective of my work and to create this book. Never would I have been able to finish such a lengthy project had I not had his expertise, help and patience to guide me.

Elfie Wilkins-Naucht's work can be found at:

La Jolla Museum of Contemporary Arts, La Jolla, CA
Princeton University Art Museum, Princeton, NJ
Arizona State University School of Art, Tempe, AZ
California Institute of the Arts, Art Library, Valencia, CA
University of Alaska, Fairbanks, Alaska
SPARC, Social and Public Arts Resource Center, Venice, CA
Roosevelt Elementary School Library, Santa Monica, CA
Hawai'i Museum of Contemporary Art, Hilo, Hawai'i
Columbia College, Chicago, IL
Museum of Contemporary Photography, Chicago, IL
Victoria Albert Museum, London, England
Georges Pompidou Centre, Paris, France
Los Angeles County Art Museum, Los Angeles, CA
On-line Archive of California
Hammer Museum, Los Angeles, CA
Pacific Tsunami Museum, Hilo, Hawai'i
The Women's Building Digital Archive, Los Angeles, CA
Grunwald Center for the Graphic Arts, Los Angeles, CA
Erie Art Center, Permanent Collection, Erie, PA

Copyright © 2015
Elfie Watkins-Nacht.
All rights reserved. No part of this publication may be reproduced, stored in any retrieval system or transmitted in any form for any means electronic, mechanical, photocopying or otherwise without first obtaining written permission from the copyright owner.

This 2015 edition published and distributed by EHCC/Hawai'i Museum of Contemporary Art
141 Kalakaua St. Hilo, Hi 96720.

Designed and edited by Lourdan Kimbrell of Lourdanart © 2000.

www.ingramcontent.com/pod-product-compliance
Lightning Source LLC
Chambersburg PA
CBHW040452220526
45473CB00004B/1609